A COMFY AND FUZZY COLORING BOOK FOR TEENS & ADULTS

COZY SPACES
AND HYGGE CORNERS

COZY SPACES
AND HYGGE CORNERS

A COMFY AND FUZZY COLORING BOOK
FOR TEENS & ADULTS

Copyright © Grace Willowfern.
All Rights Reserved.

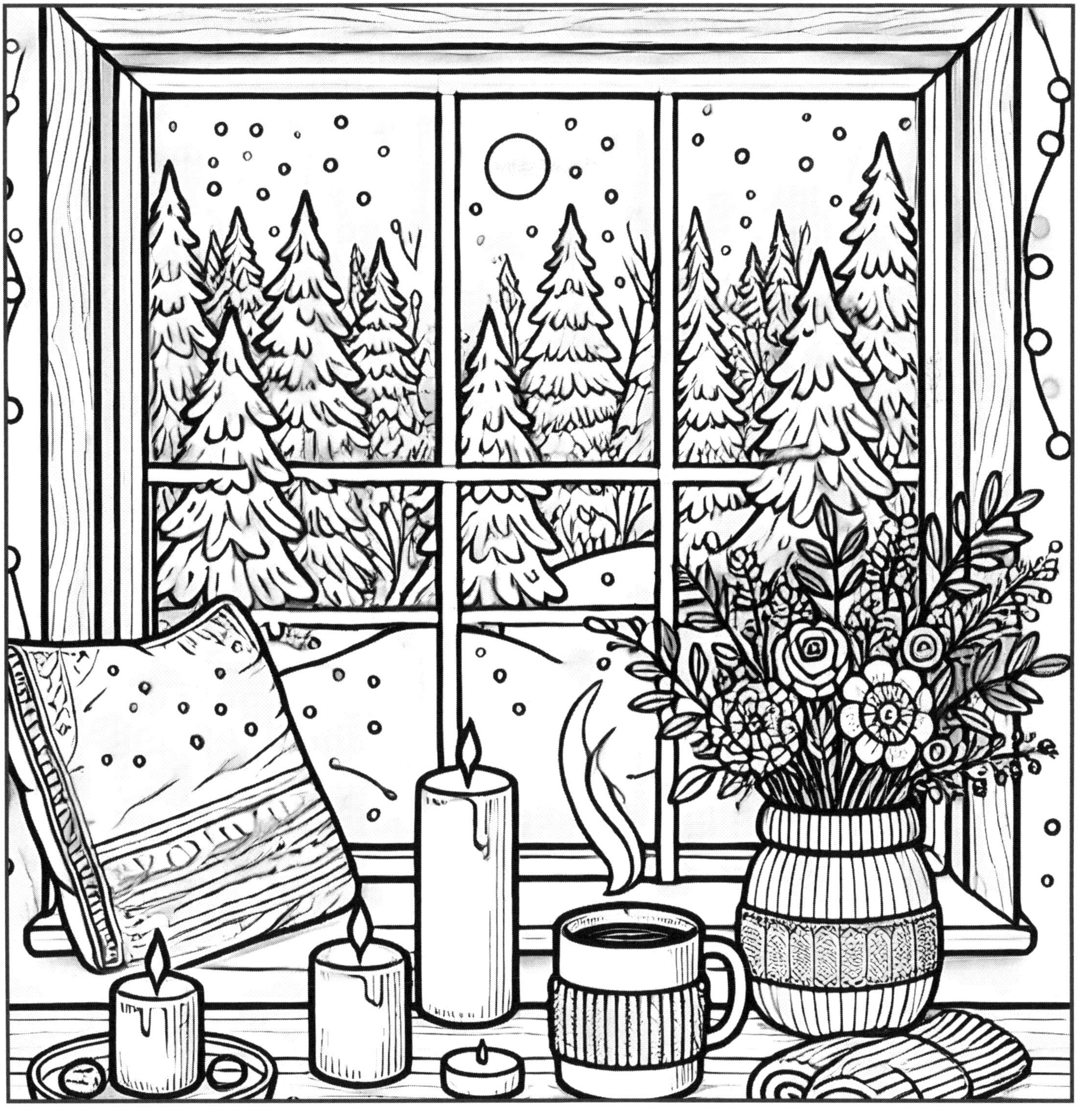

THIS BLACK PAGE IS INTENTIONALLY PLACED TO ENSURE NO BLEED-THROUGH TO THE NEXT PAGE.

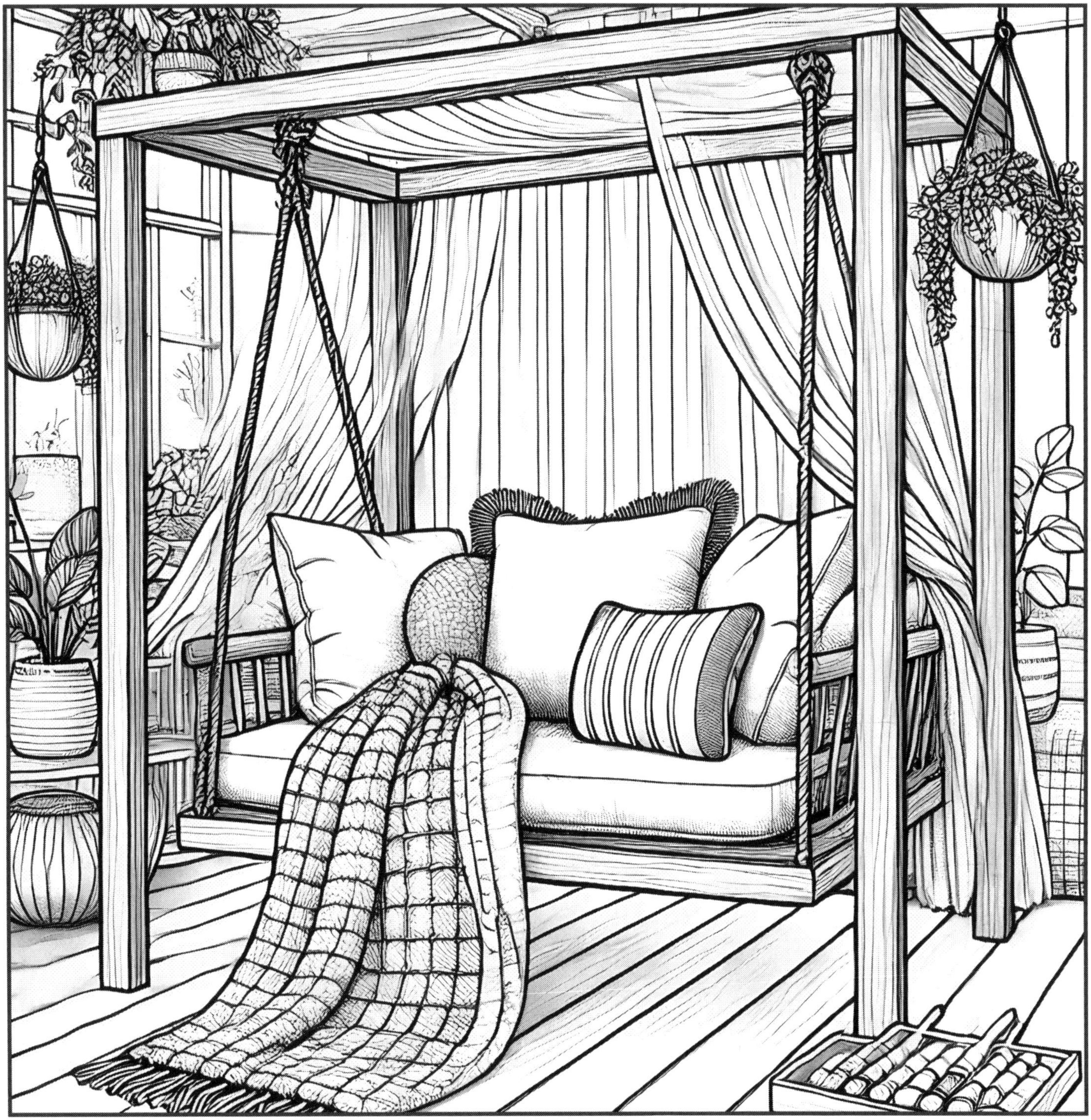

THIS BLACK PAGE IS INTENTIONALLY PLACED TO ENSURE NO BLEED-THROUGH TO THE NEXT PAGE.

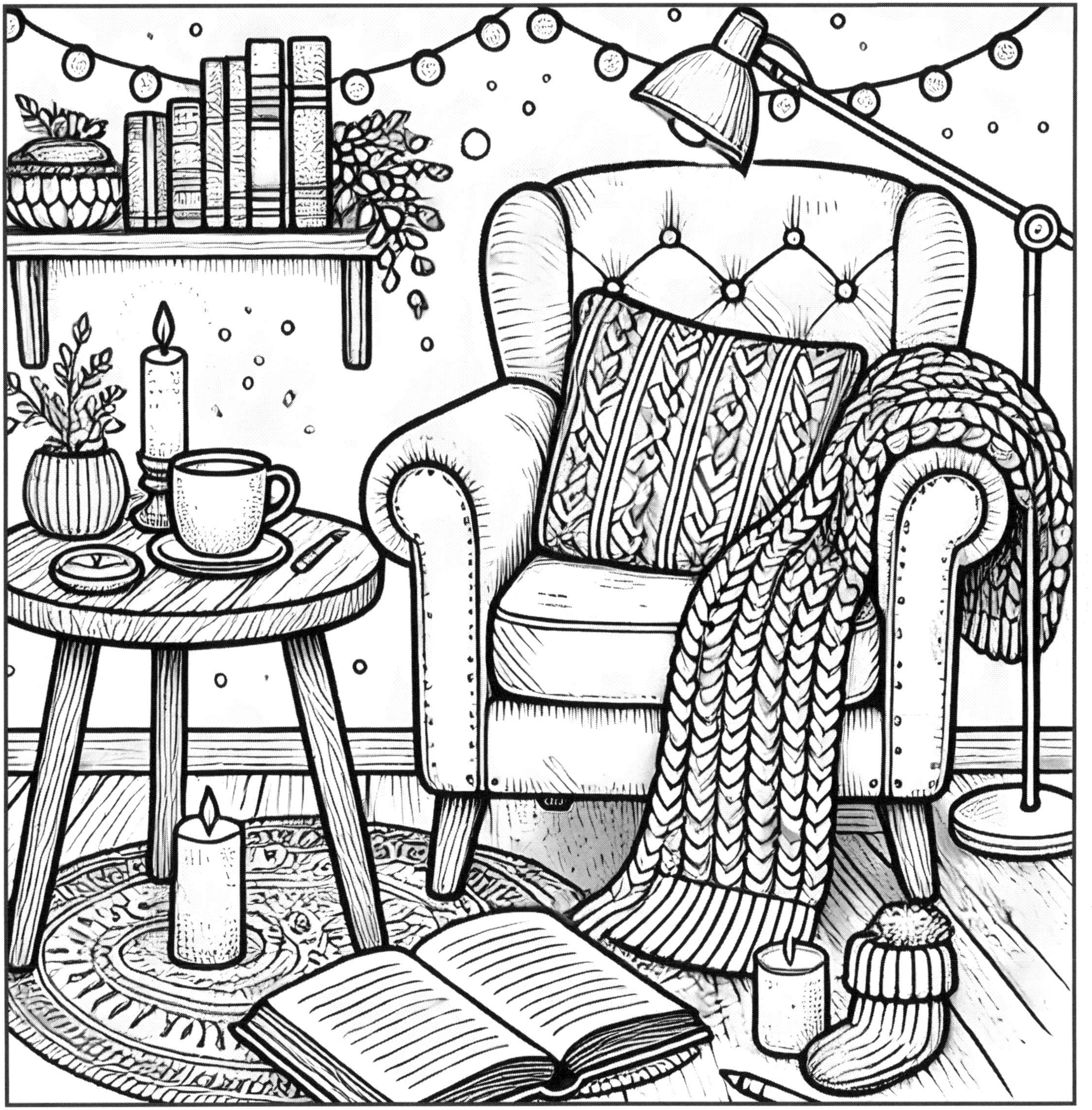

THIS BLACK PAGE IS INTENTIONALLY PLACED TO ENSURE NO BLEED-THROUGH TO THE NEXT PAGE.

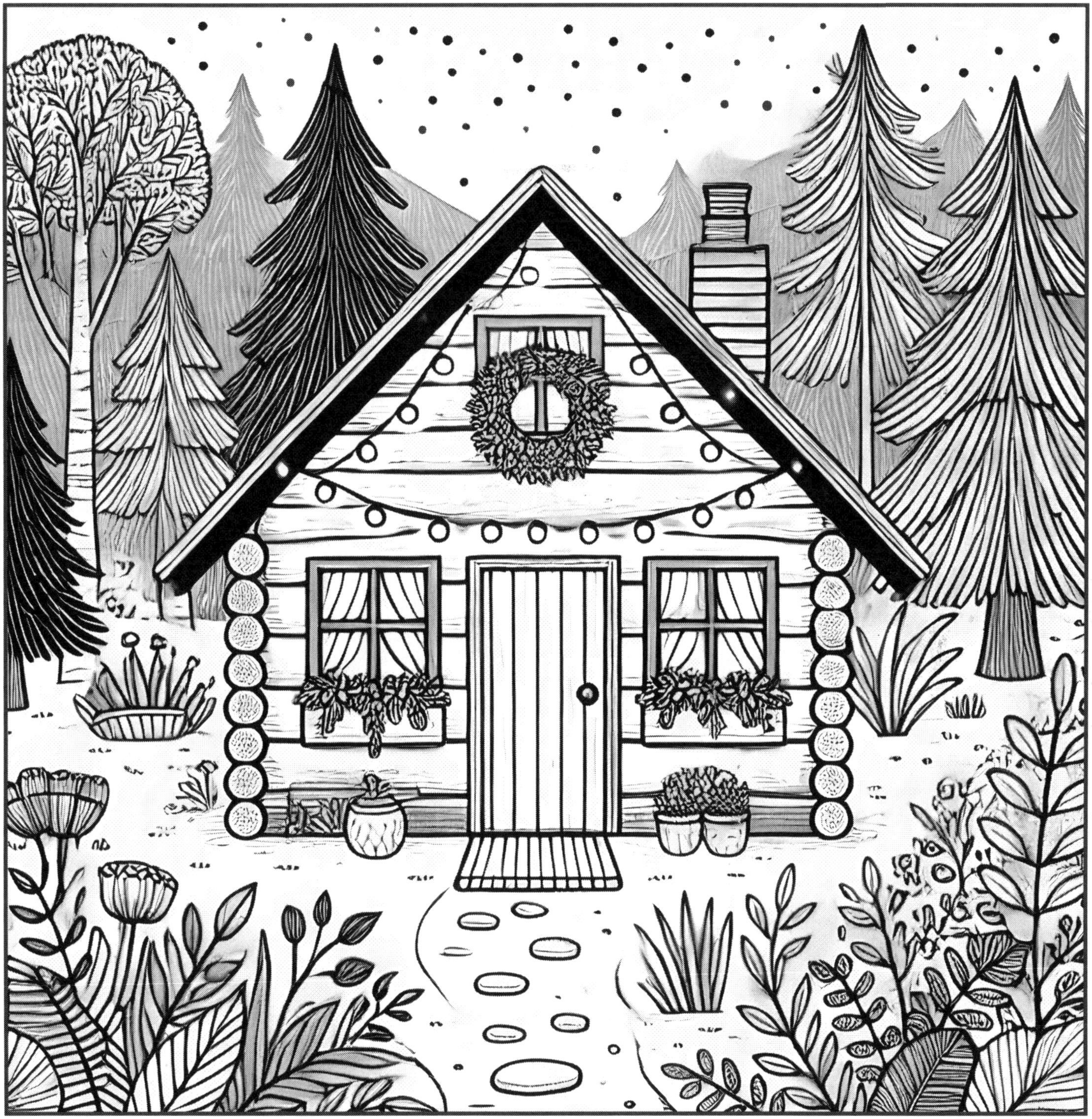

THIS BLACK PAGE IS INTENTIONALLY PLACED TO ENSURE NO BLEED-THROUGH TO THE NEXT PAGE.

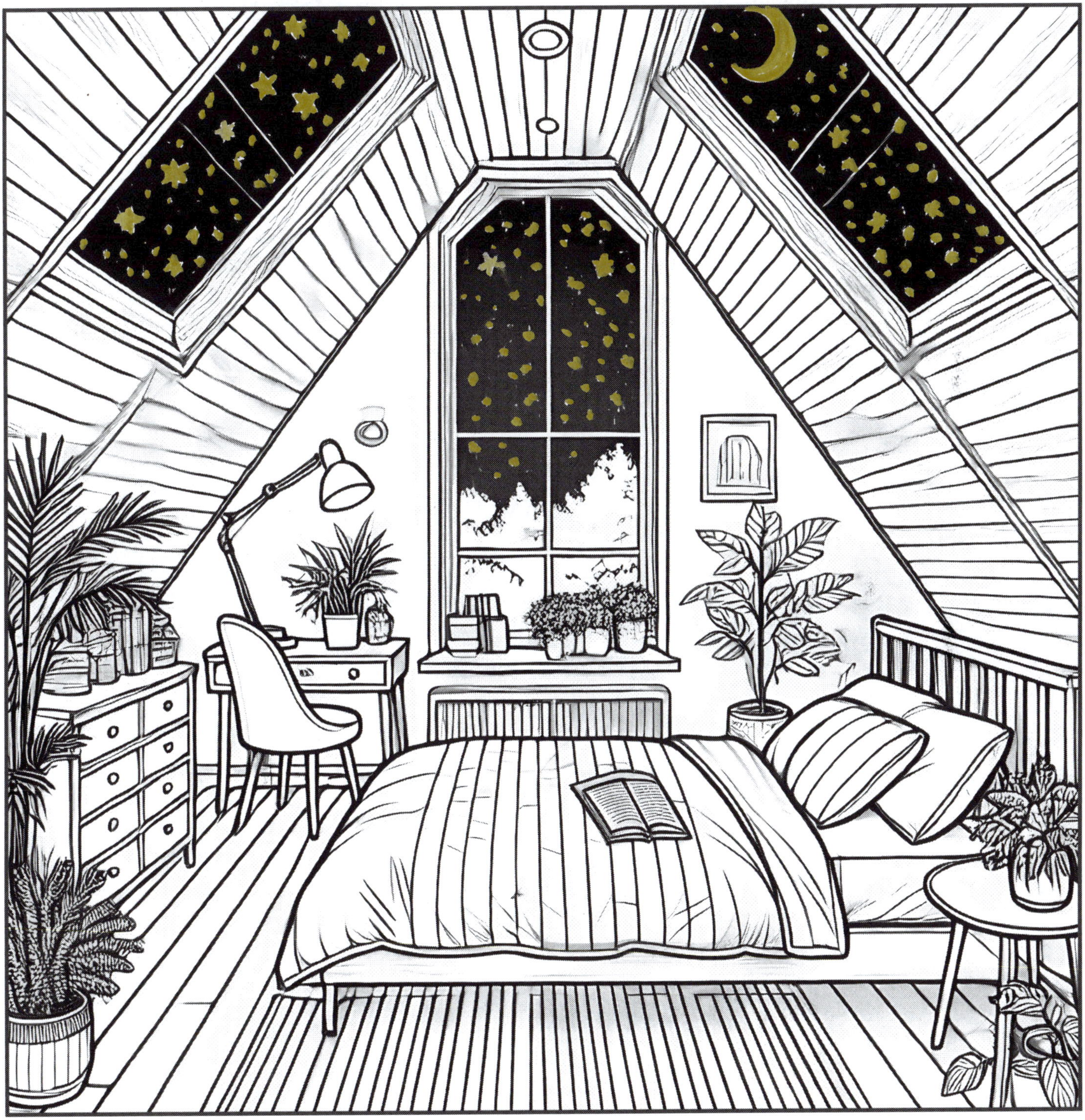

THIS BLACK PAGE IS INTENTIONALLY PLACED TO ENSURE NO BLEED-THROUGH TO THE NEXT PAGE.

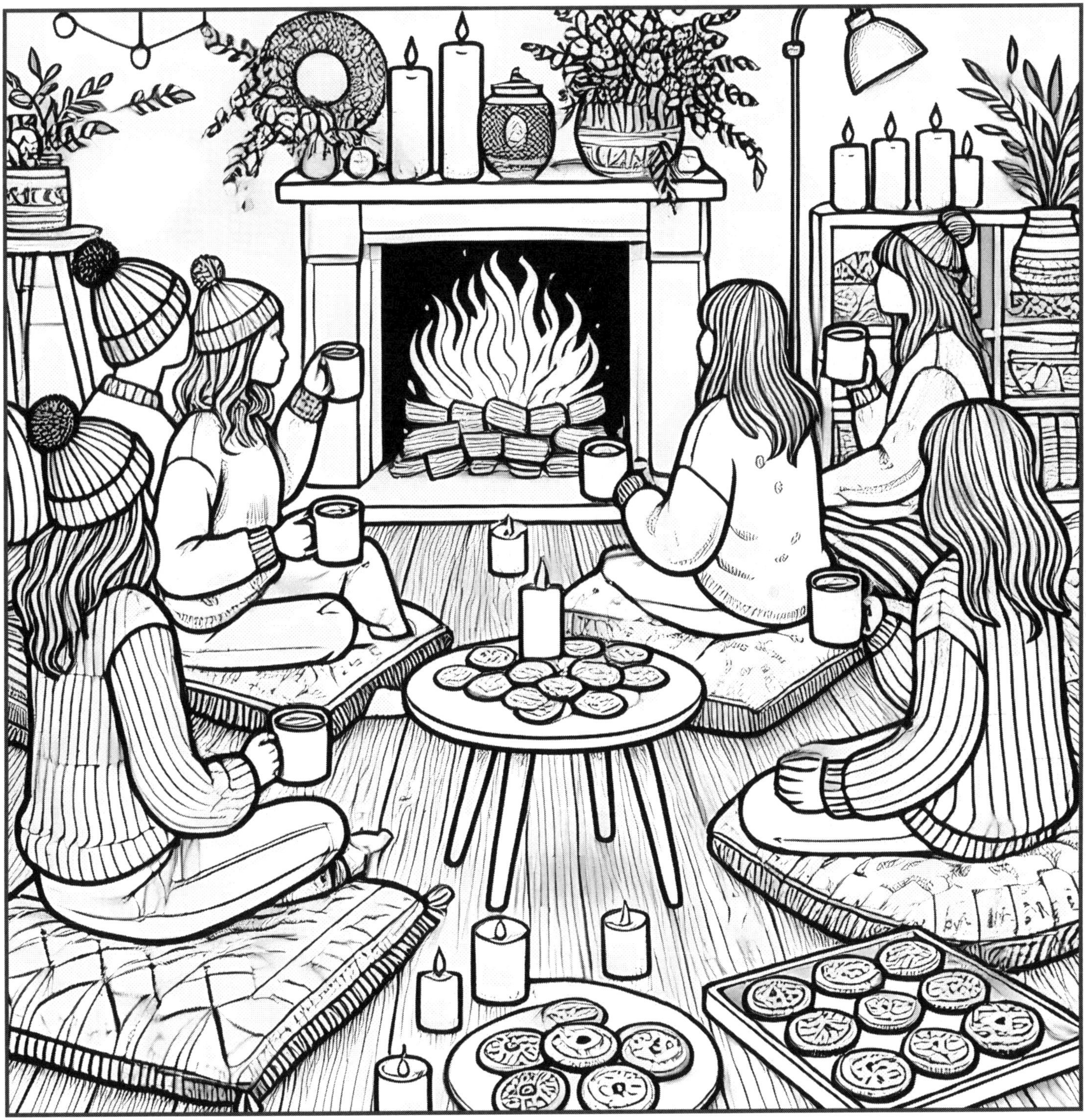

THIS BLACK PAGE IS INTENTIONALLY PLACED TO
ENSURE NO BLEED-THROUGH TO THE NEXT PAGE.

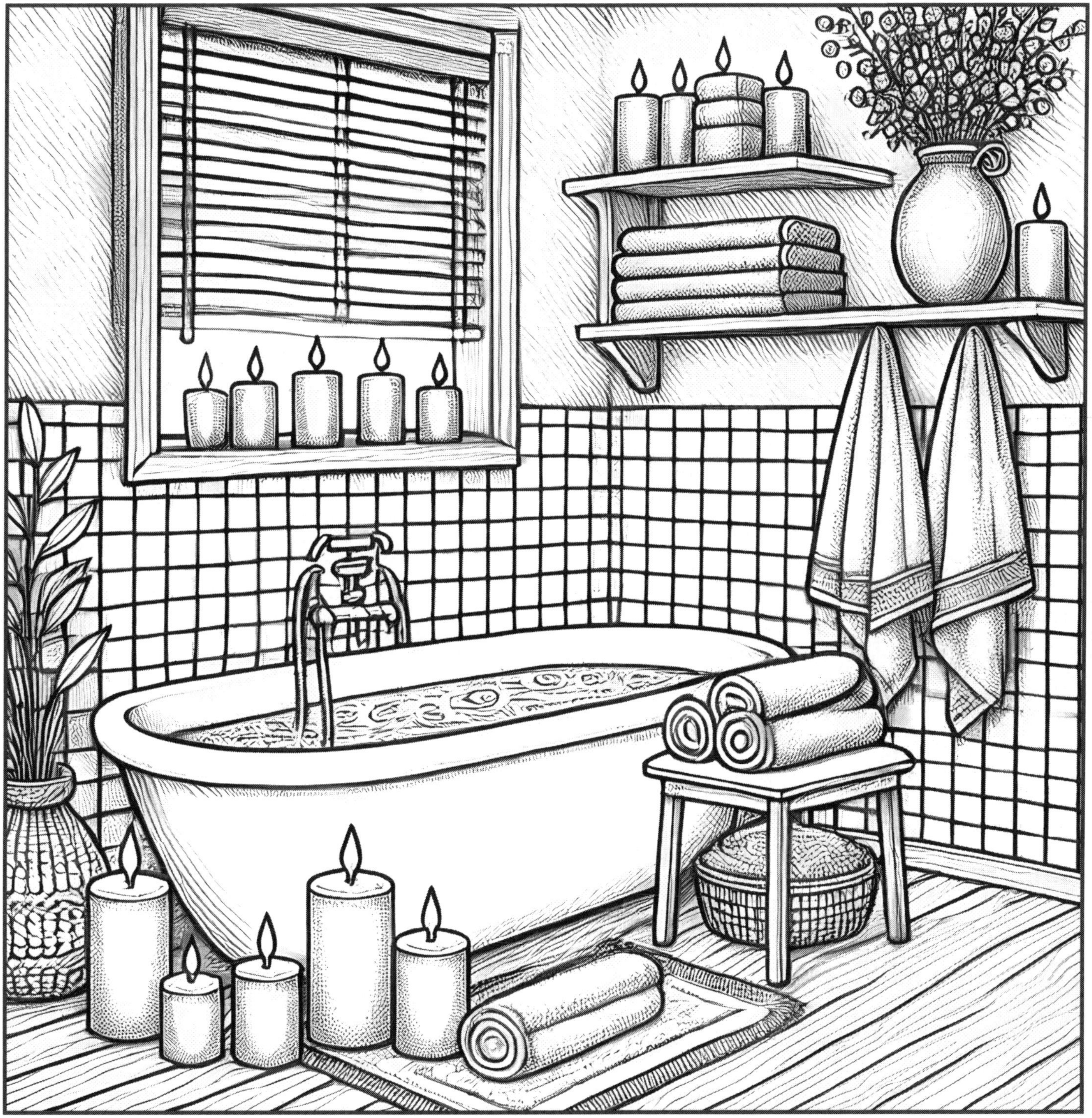

THIS BLACK PAGE IS INTENTIONALLY PLACED TO ENSURE NO BLEED-THROUGH TO THE NEXT PAGE.

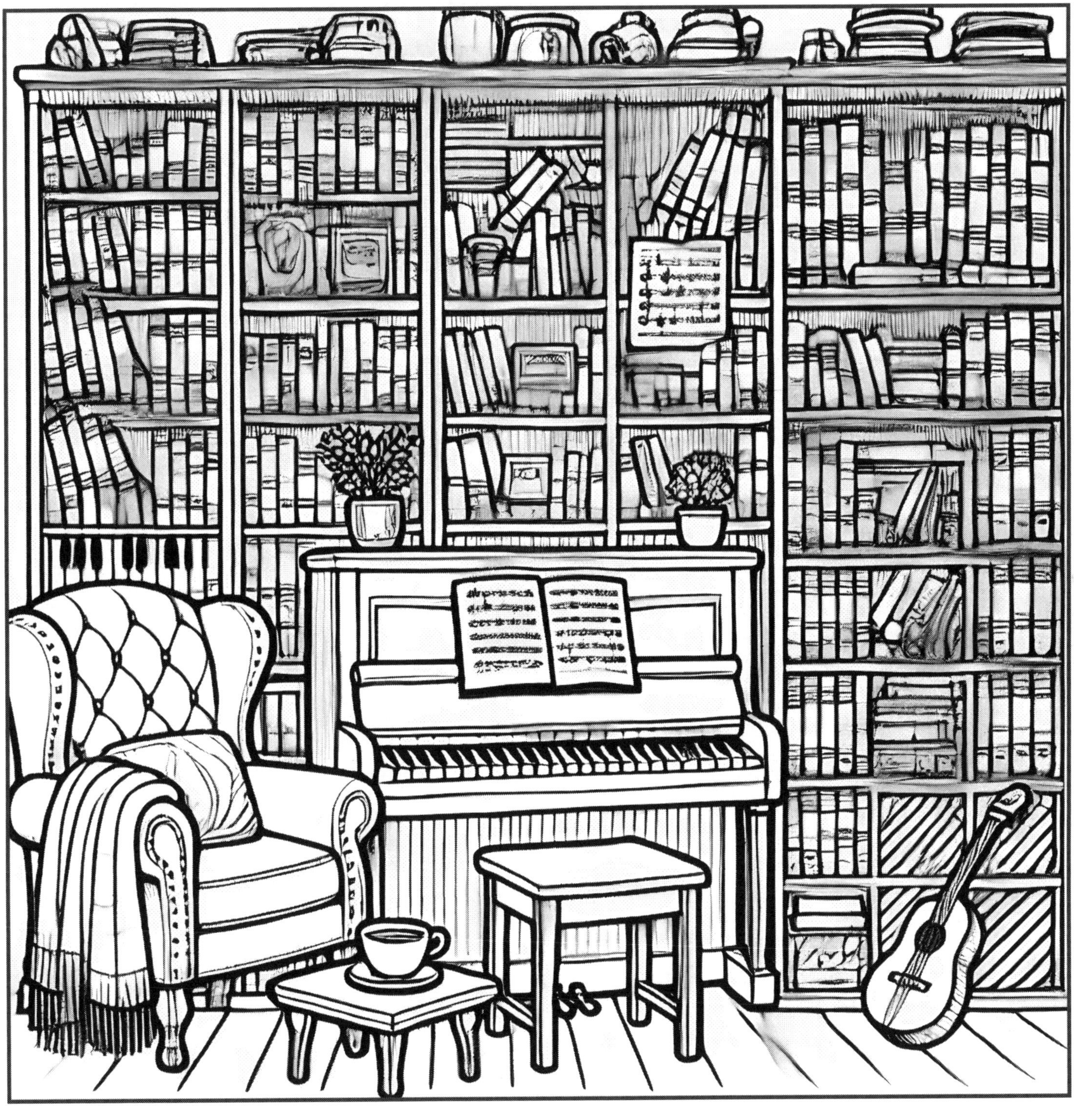

THIS BLACK PAGE IS INTENTIONALLY PLACED TO ENSURE NO BLEED-THROUGH TO THE NEXT PAGE.

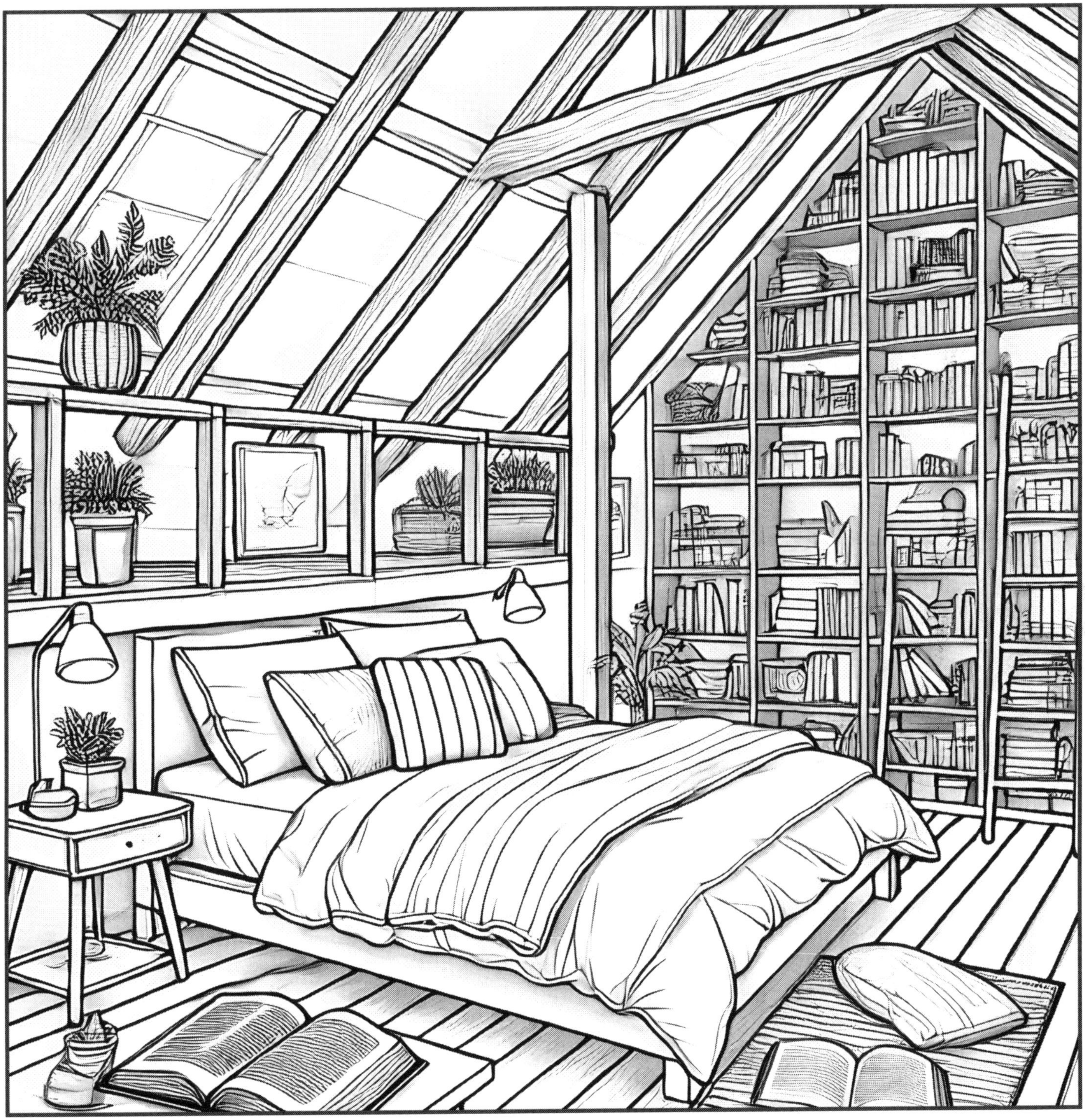

THIS BLACK PAGE IS INTENTIONALLY PLACED TO ENSURE NO BLEED-THROUGH TO THE NEXT PAGE.

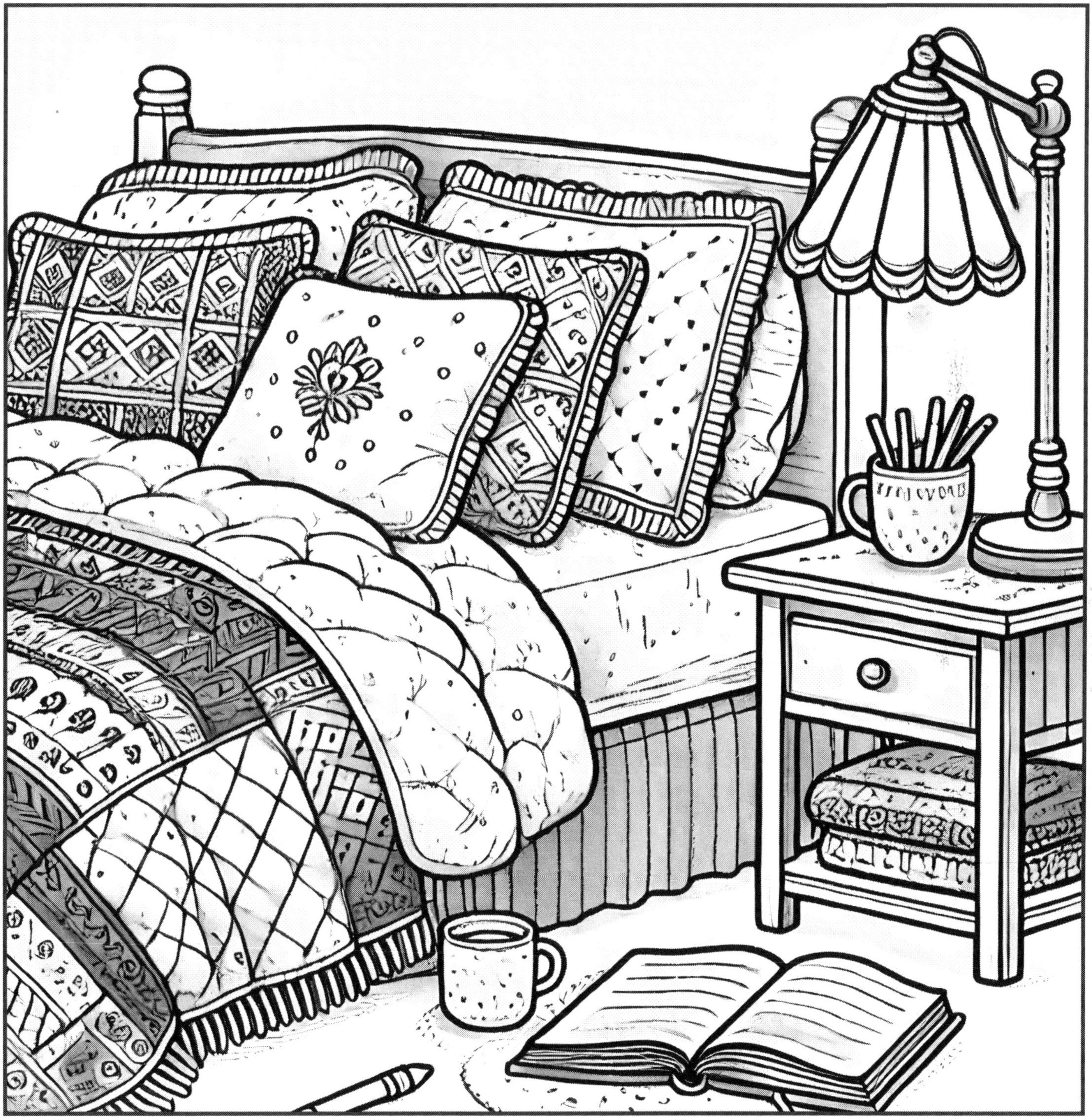

THIS BLACK PAGE IS INTENTIONALLY PLACED TO
ENSURE NO BLEED-THROUGH TO THE NEXT PAGE.

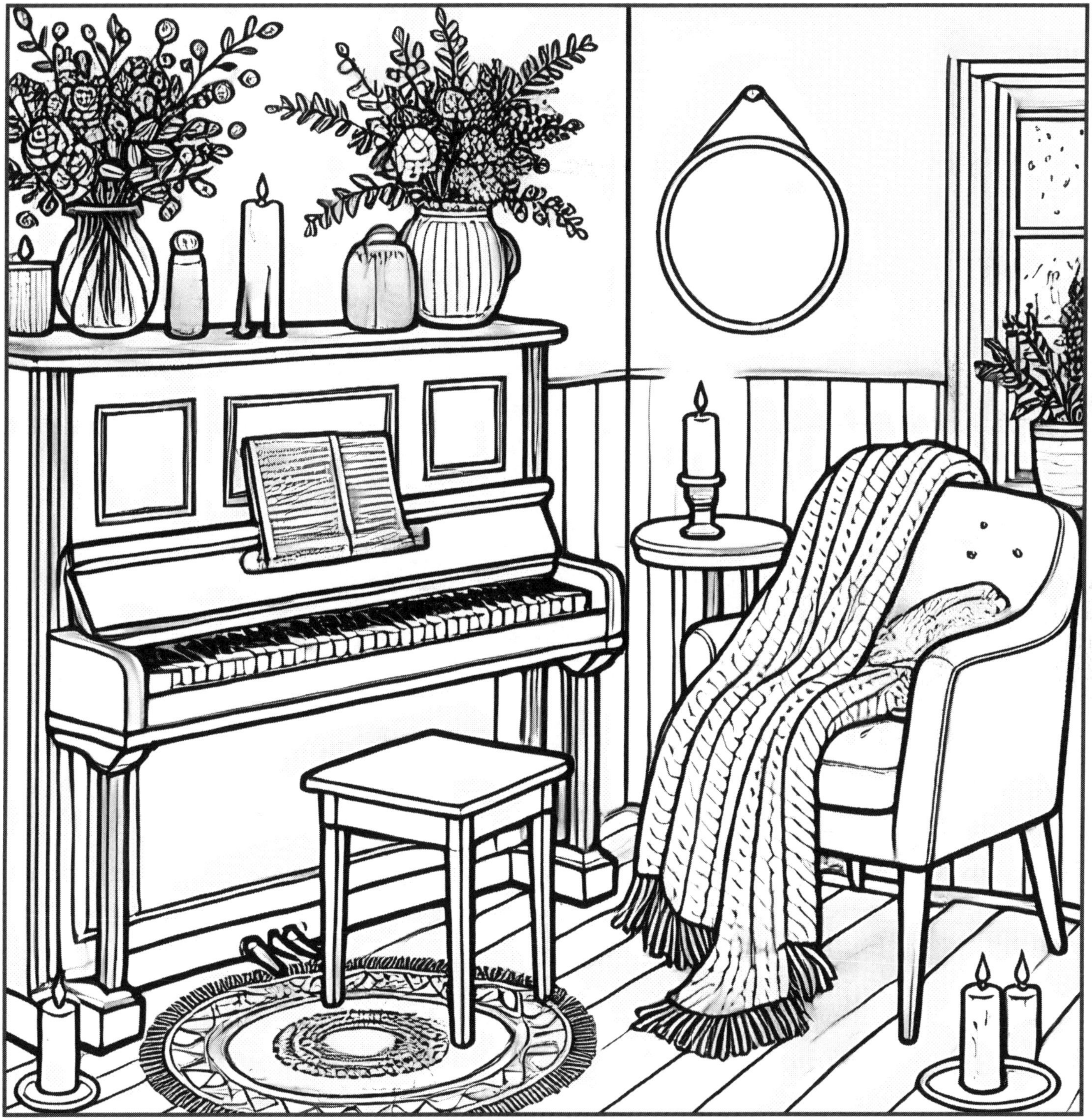

THIS BLACK PAGE IS INTENTIONALLY PLACED TO ENSURE NO BLEED-THROUGH TO THE NEXT PAGE.

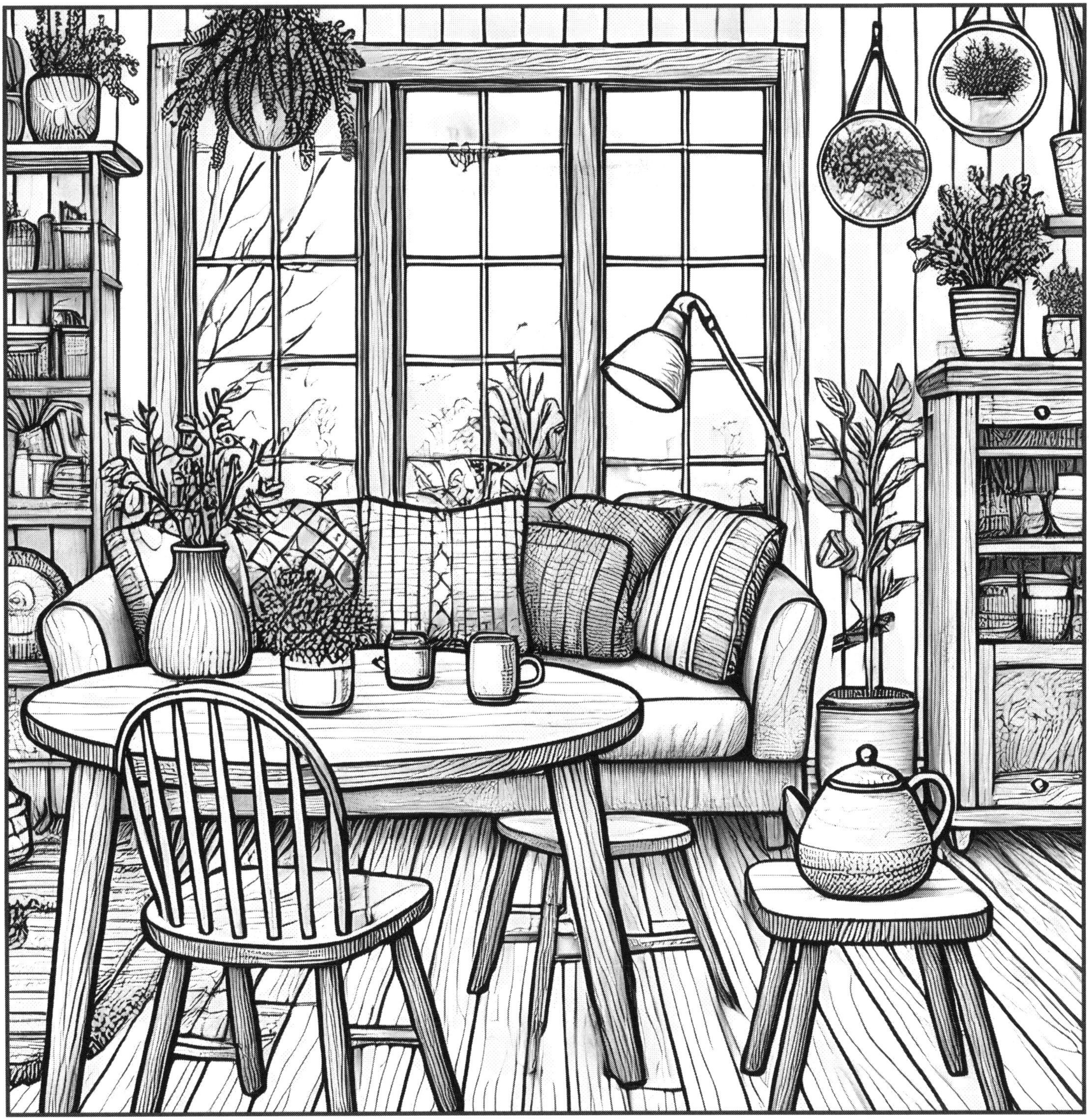

THIS BLACK PAGE IS INTENTIONALLY PLACED TO
ENSURE NO BLEED-THROUGH TO THE NEXT PAGE.

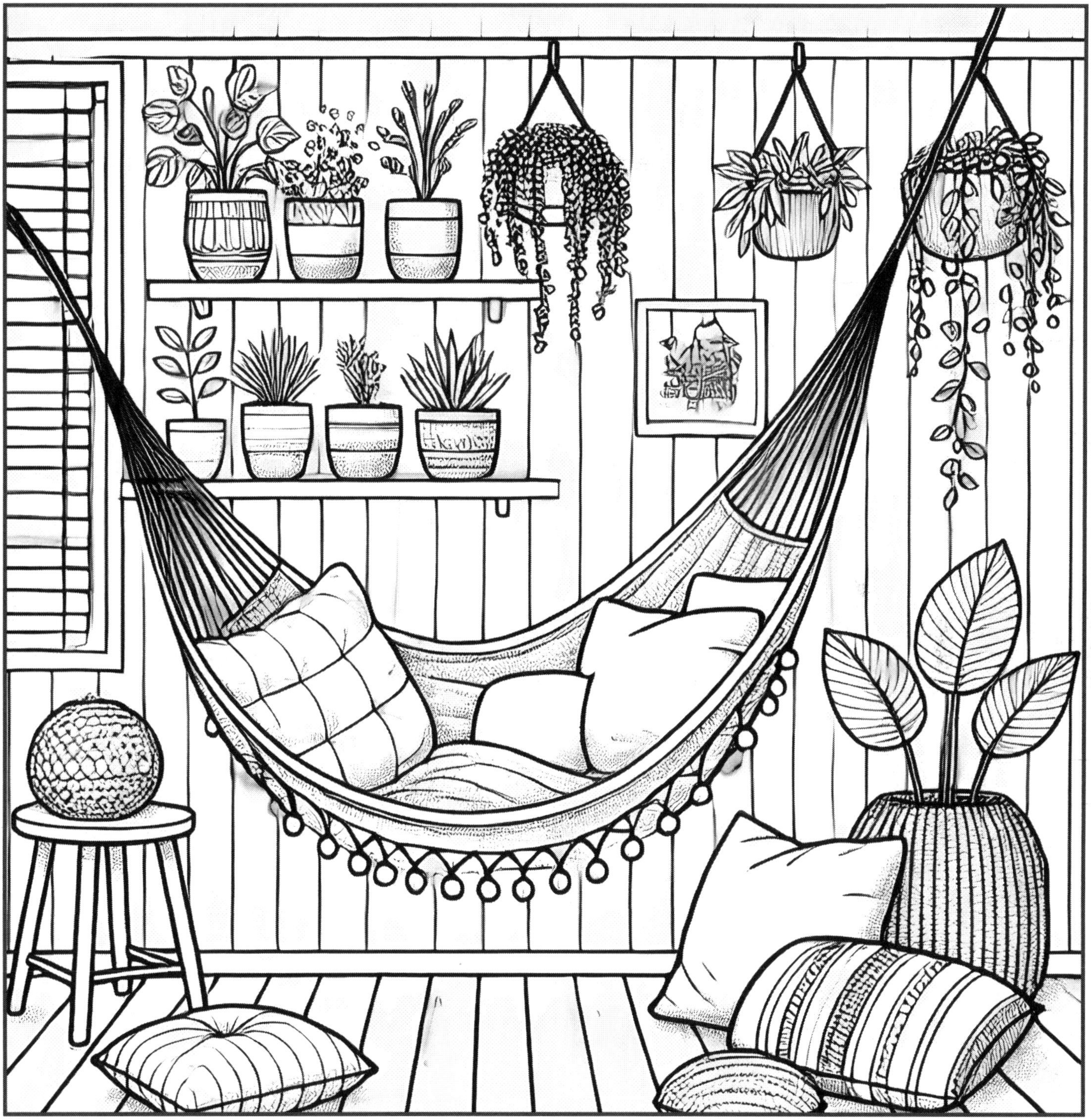

THIS BLACK PAGE IS INTENTIONALLY PLACED TO ENSURE NO BLEED-THROUGH TO THE NEXT PAGE.

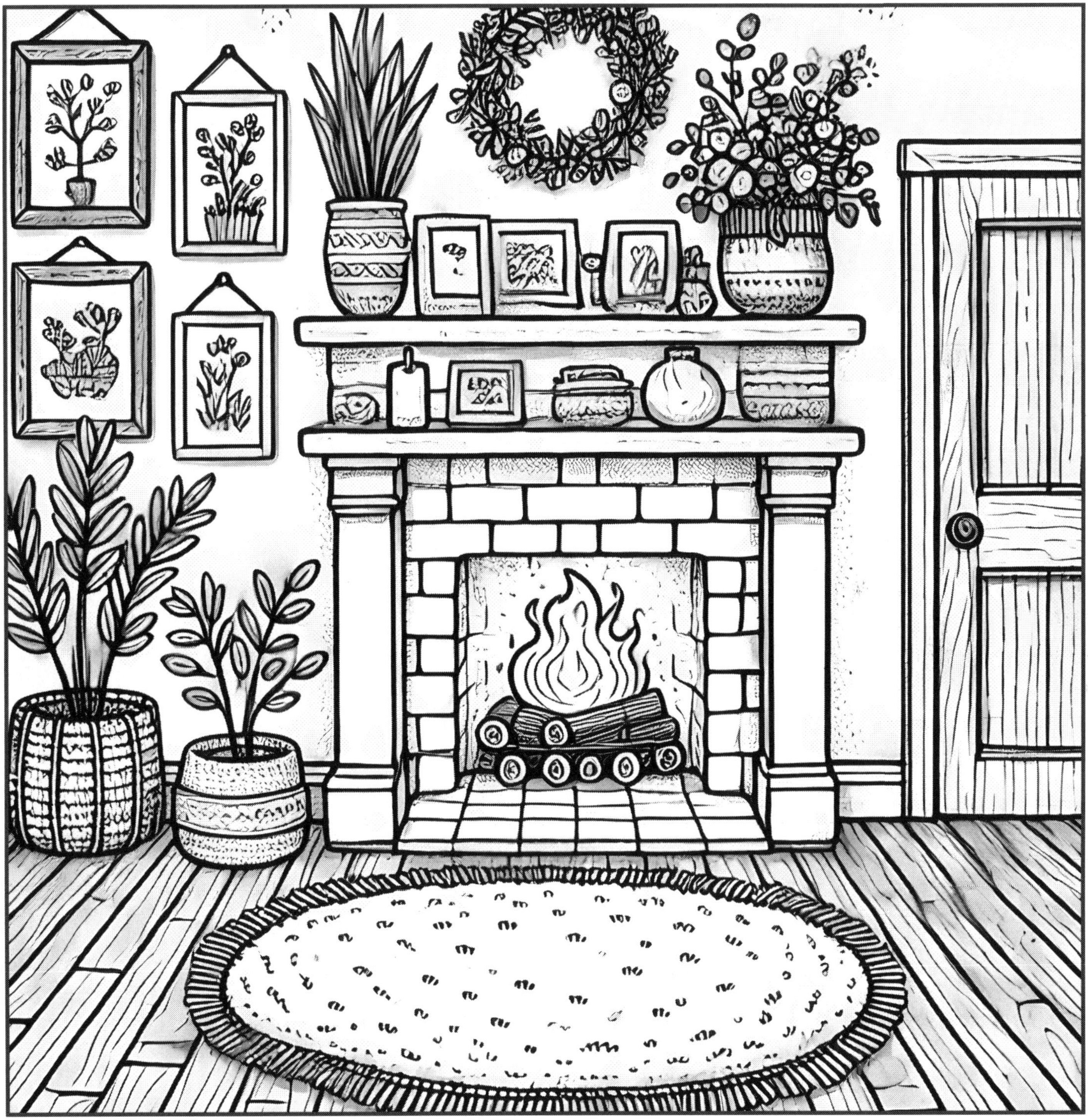

THIS BLACK PAGE IS INTENTIONALLY PLACED TO ENSURE NO BLEED-THROUGH TO THE NEXT PAGE.

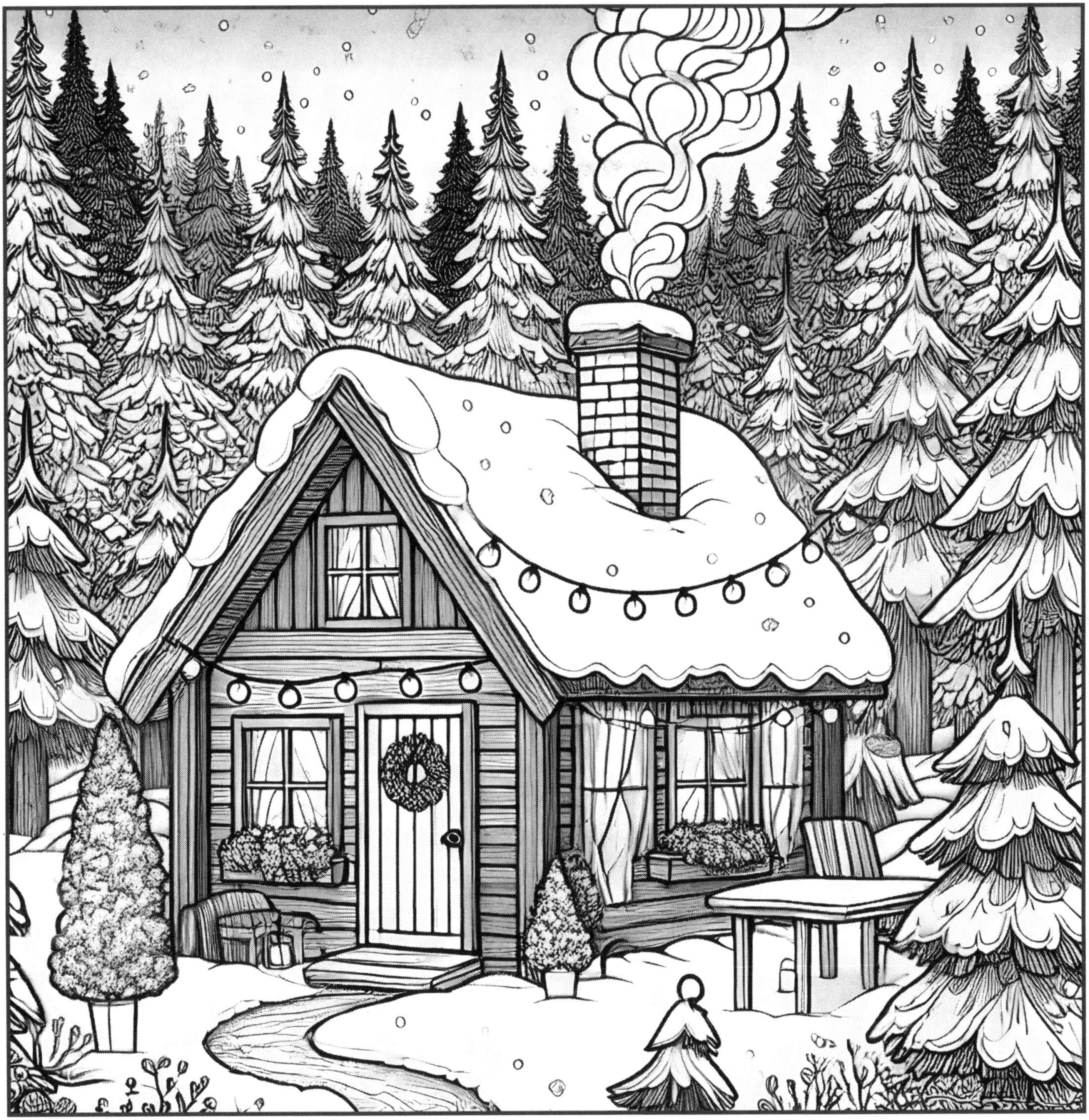

THIS BLACK PAGE IS INTENTIONALLY PLACED TO ENSURE NO BLEED-THROUGH TO THE NEXT PAGE.

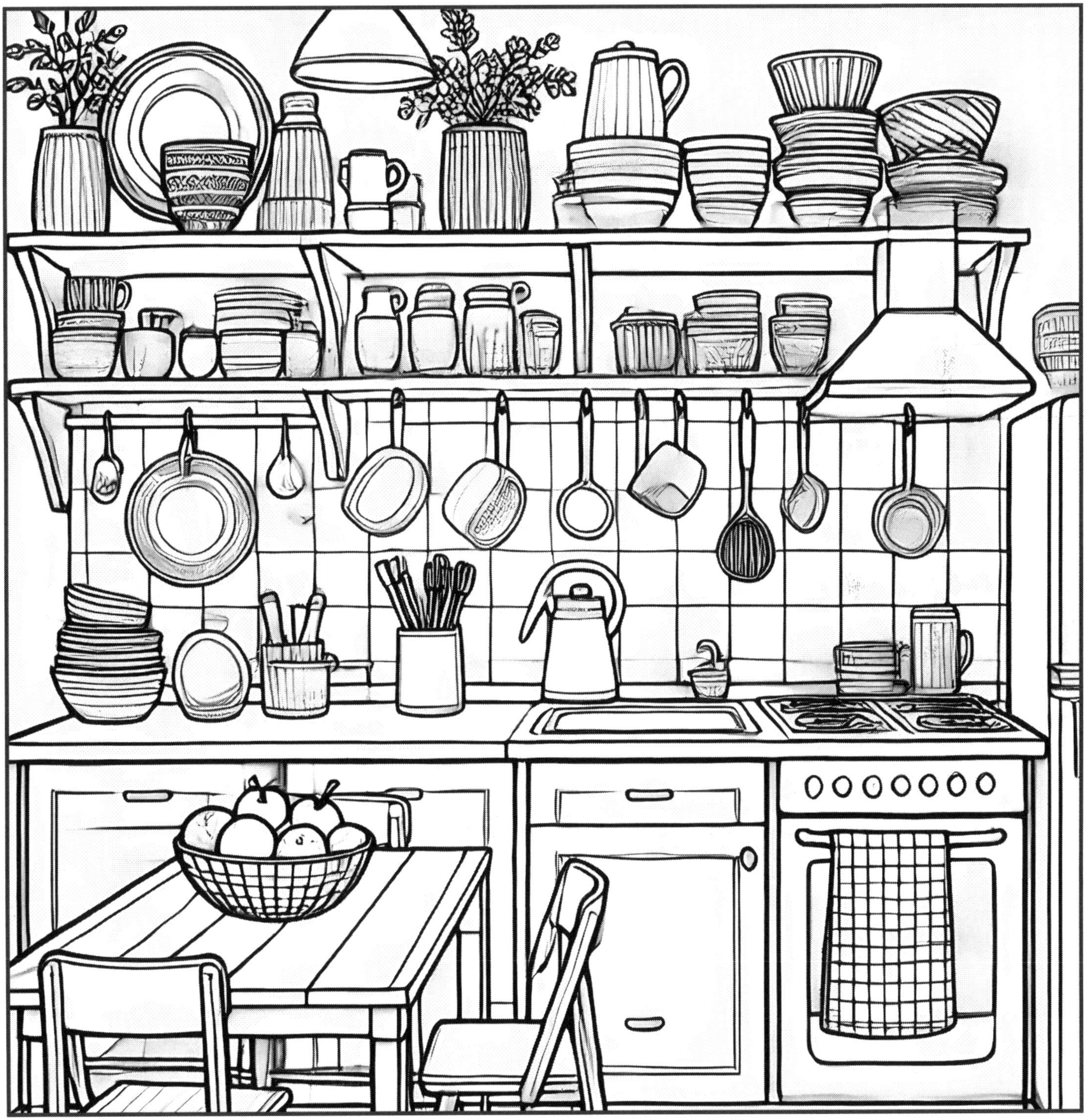

THIS BLACK PAGE IS INTENTIONALLY PLACED TO ENSURE NO BLEED-THROUGH TO THE NEXT PAGE.

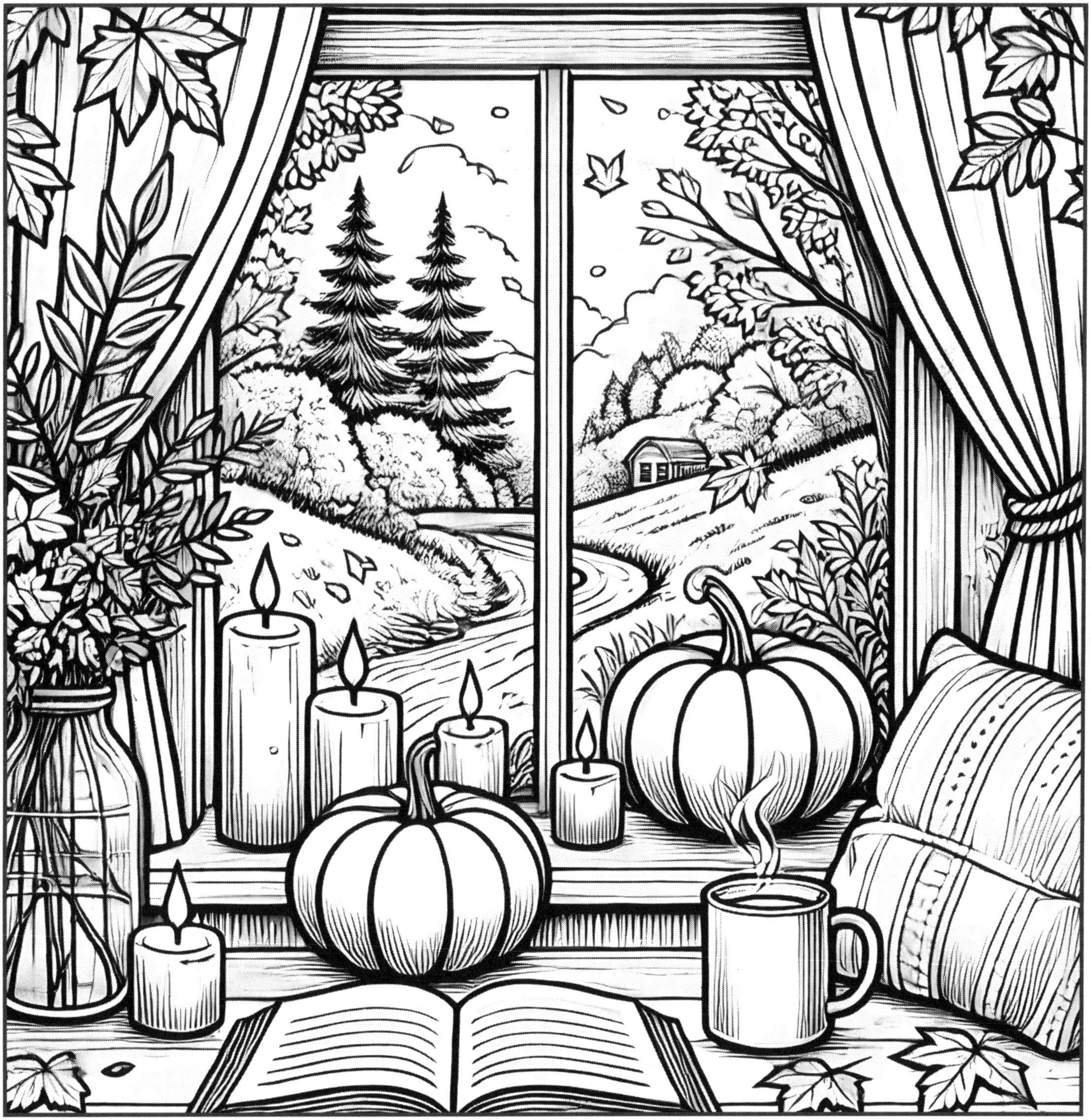

THIS BLACK PAGE IS INTENTIONALLY PLACED TO
ENSURE NO BLEED-THROUGH TO THE NEXT PAGE.

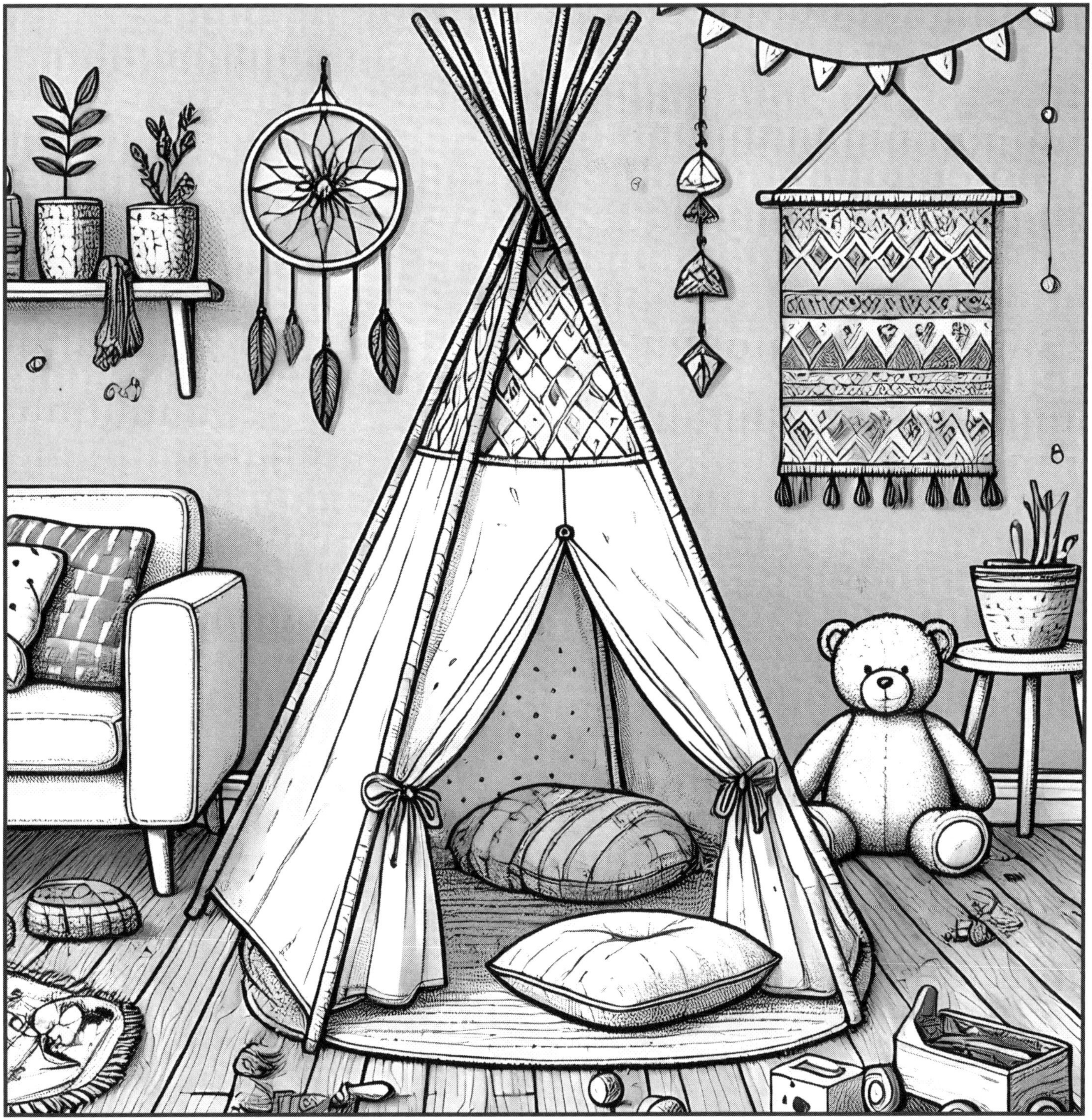

THIS BLACK PAGE IS INTENTIONALLY PLACED TO ENSURE NO BLEED-THROUGH TO THE NEXT PAGE.

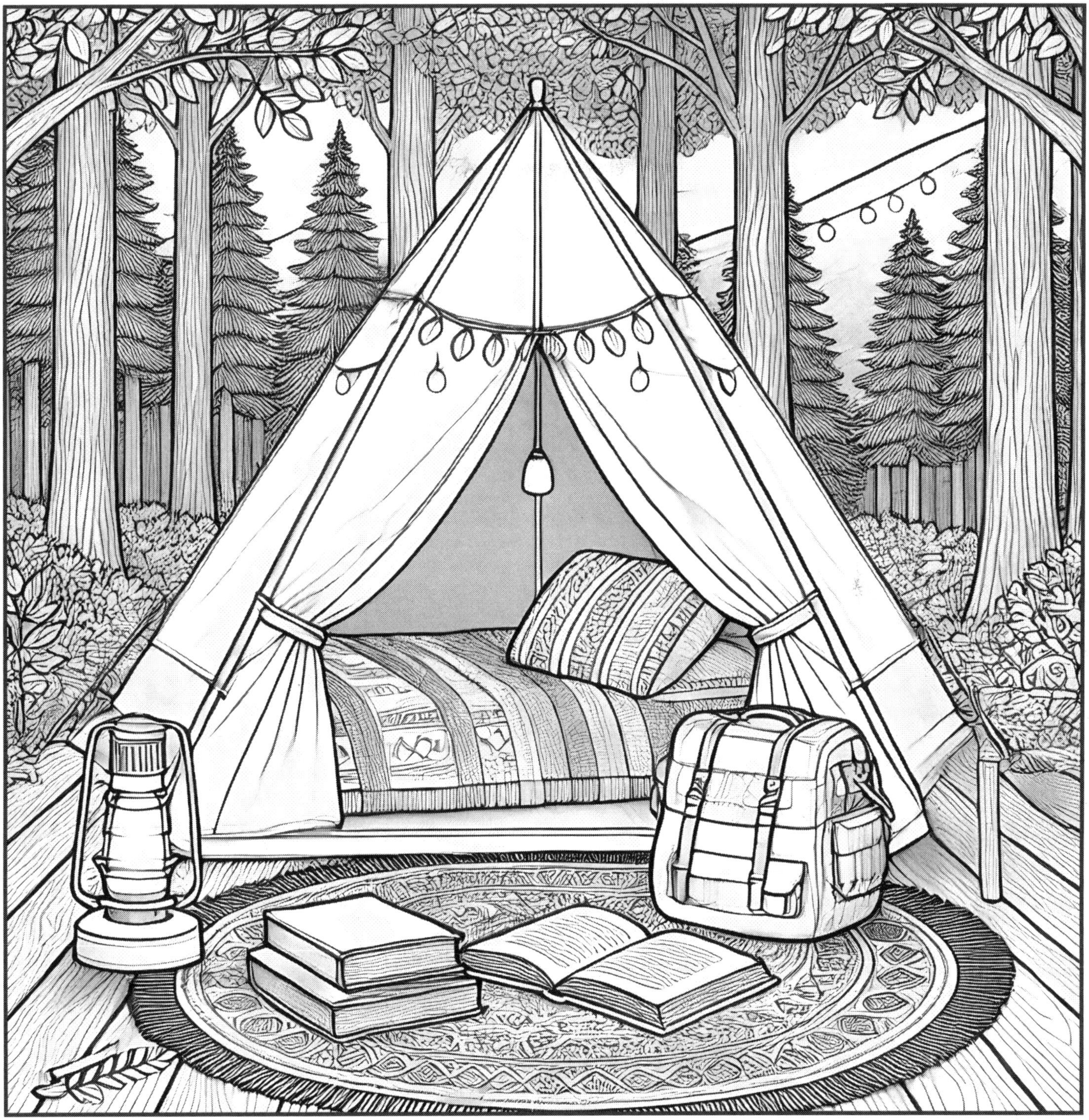

THIS BLACK PAGE IS INTENTIONALLY PLACED TO ENSURE NO BLEED-THROUGH TO THE NEXT PAGE.

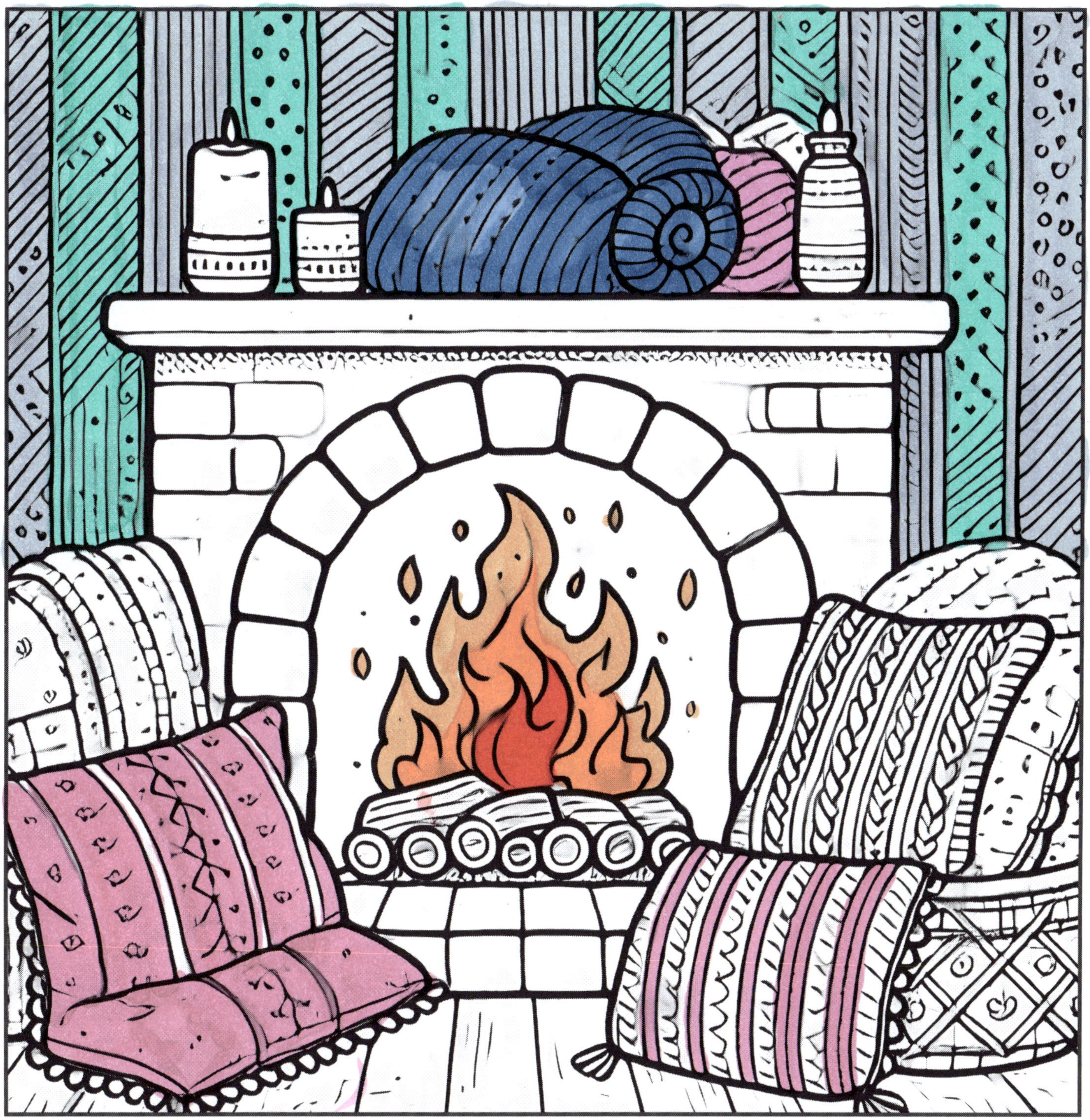

THIS BLACK PAGE IS INTENTIONALLY PLACED TO
ENSURE NO BLEED-THROUGH TO THE NEXT PAGE.

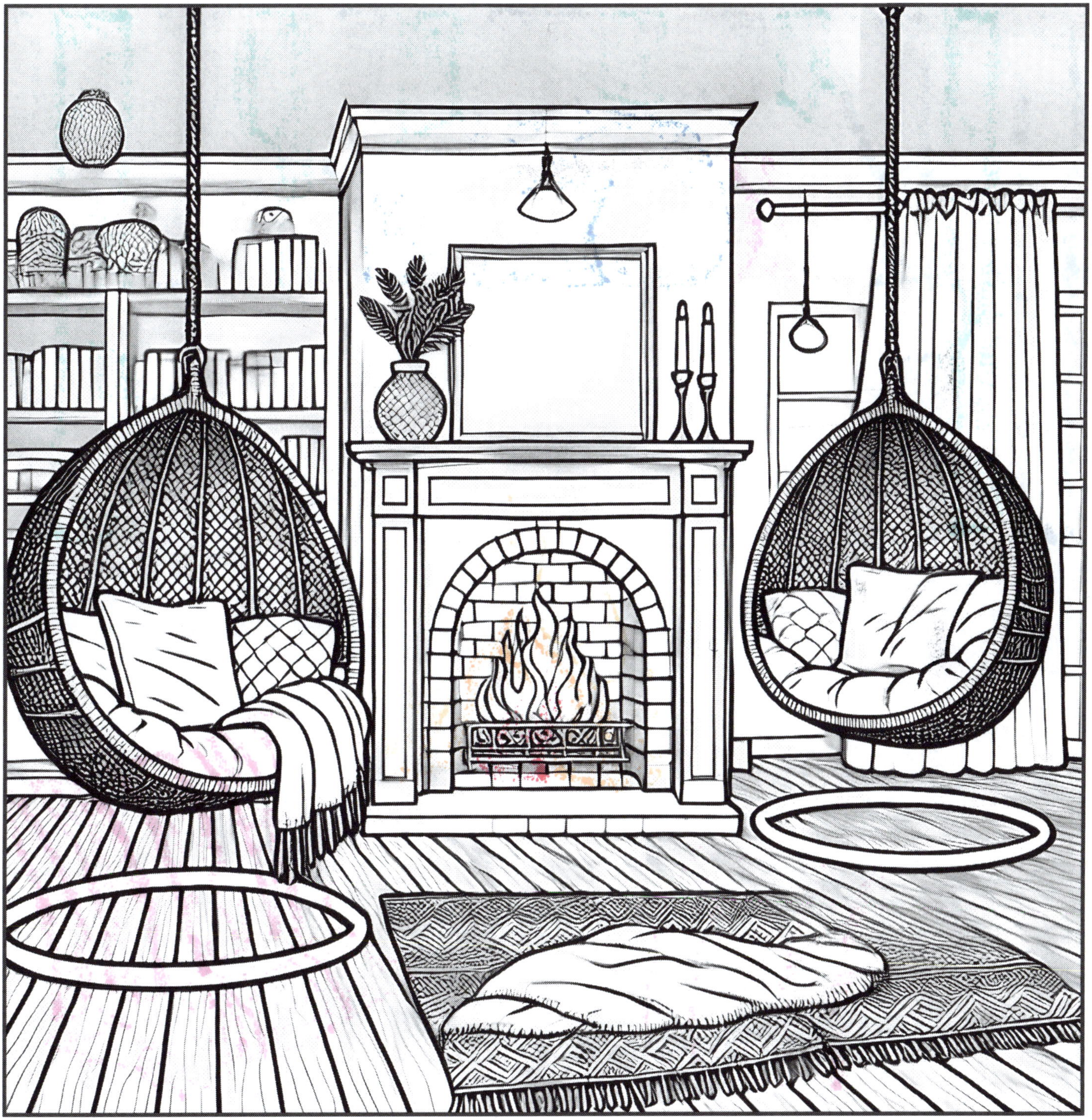

THIS BLACK PAGE IS INTENTIONALLY PLACED TO ENSURE NO BLEED-THROUGH TO THE NEXT PAGE.

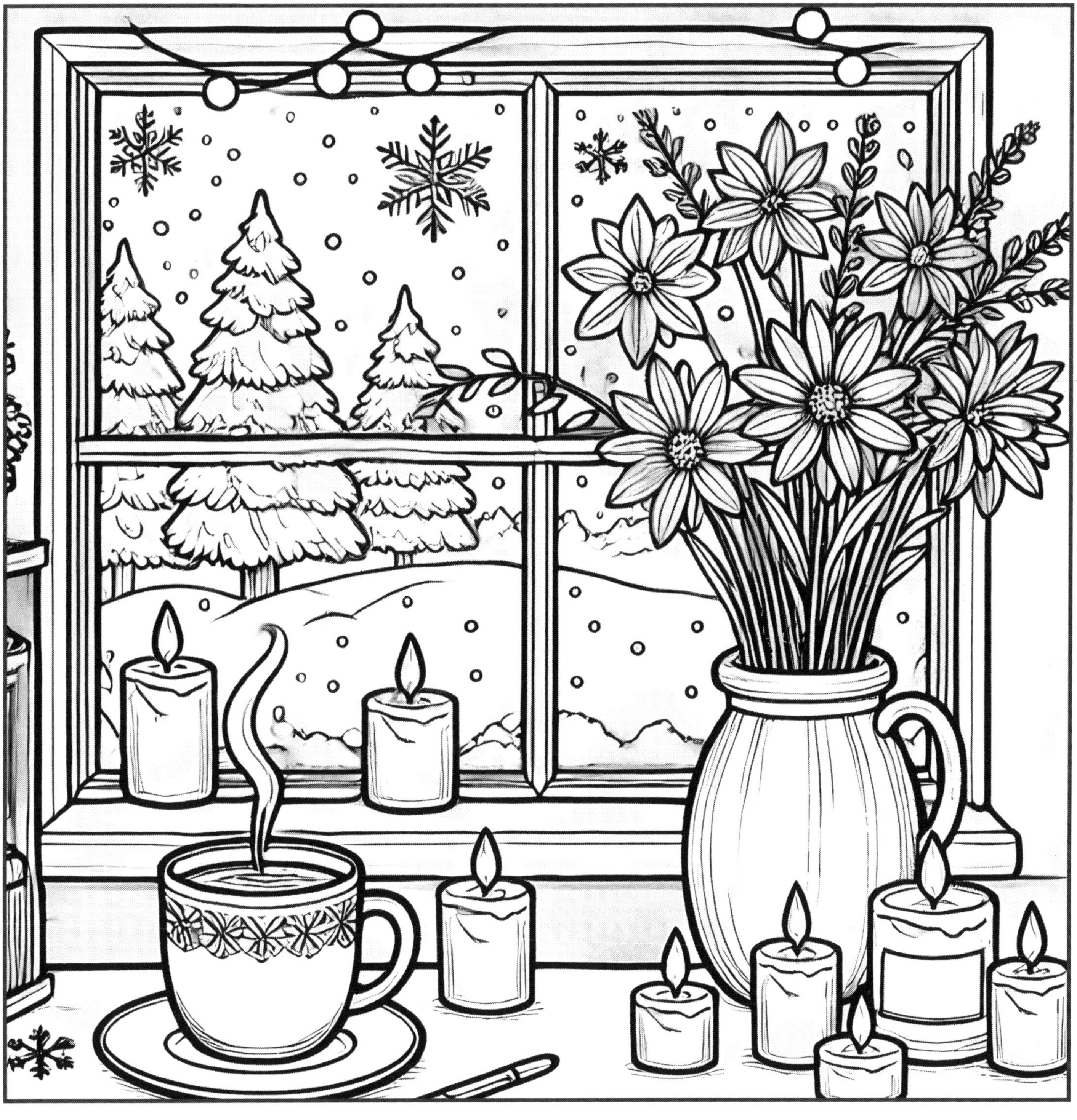

THIS BLACK PAGE IS INTENTIONALLY PLACED TO ENSURE NO BLEED-THROUGH TO THE NEXT PAGE.

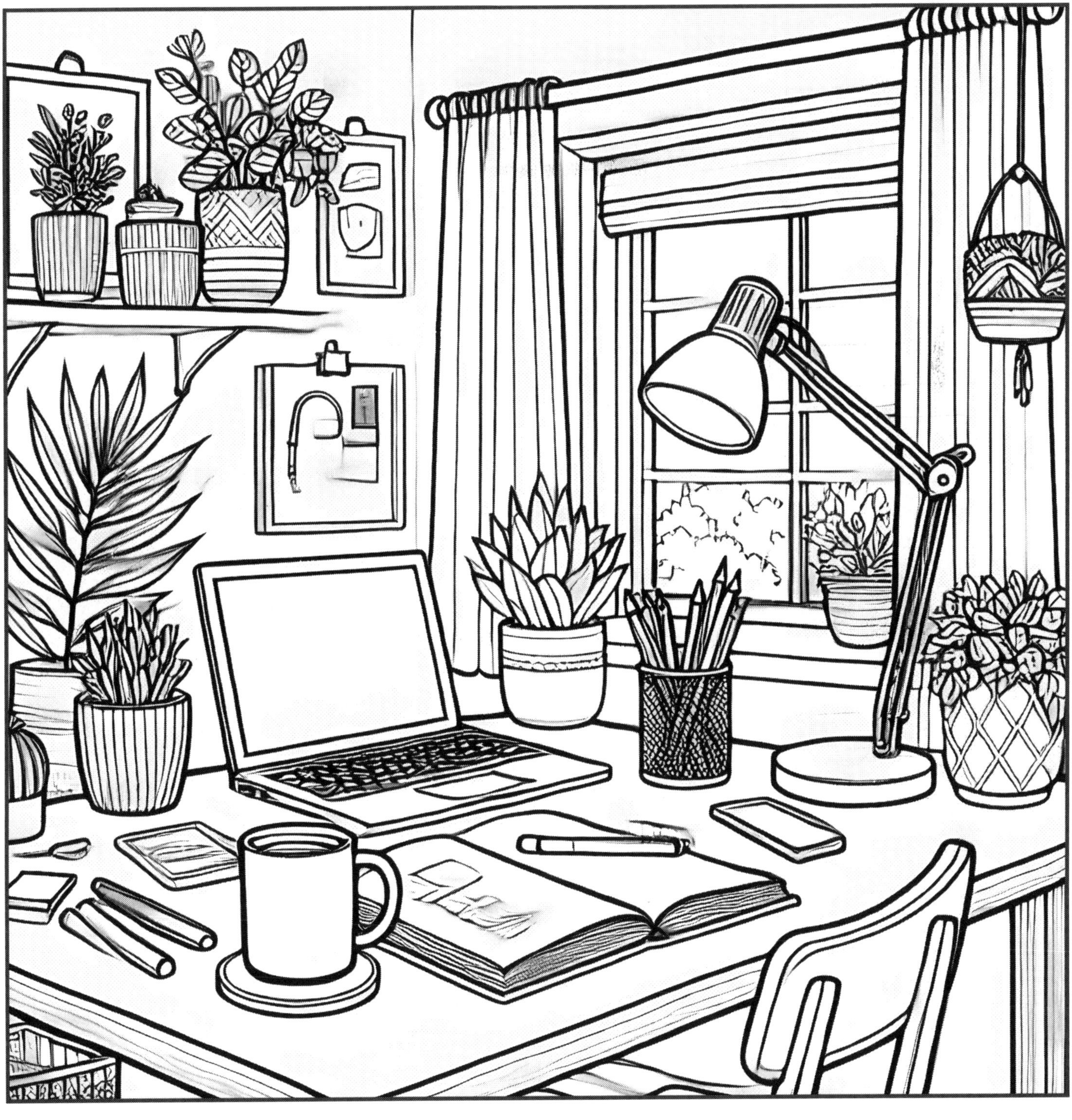

THIS BLACK PAGE IS INTENTIONALLY PLACED TO ENSURE NO BLEED-THROUGH TO THE NEXT PAGE.

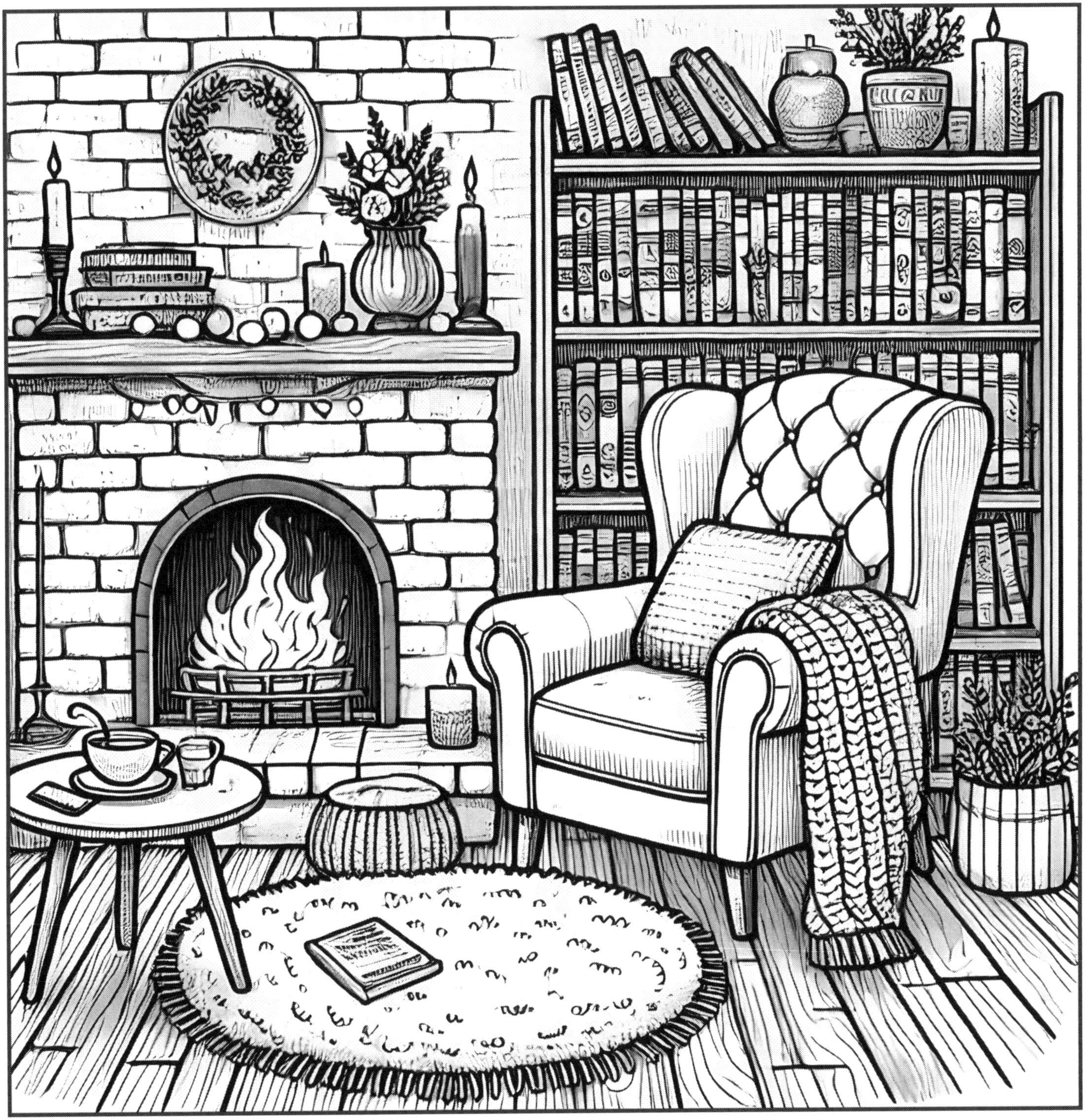

THIS BLACK PAGE IS INTENTIONALLY PLACED TO ENSURE NO BLEED-THROUGH TO THE NEXT PAGE.

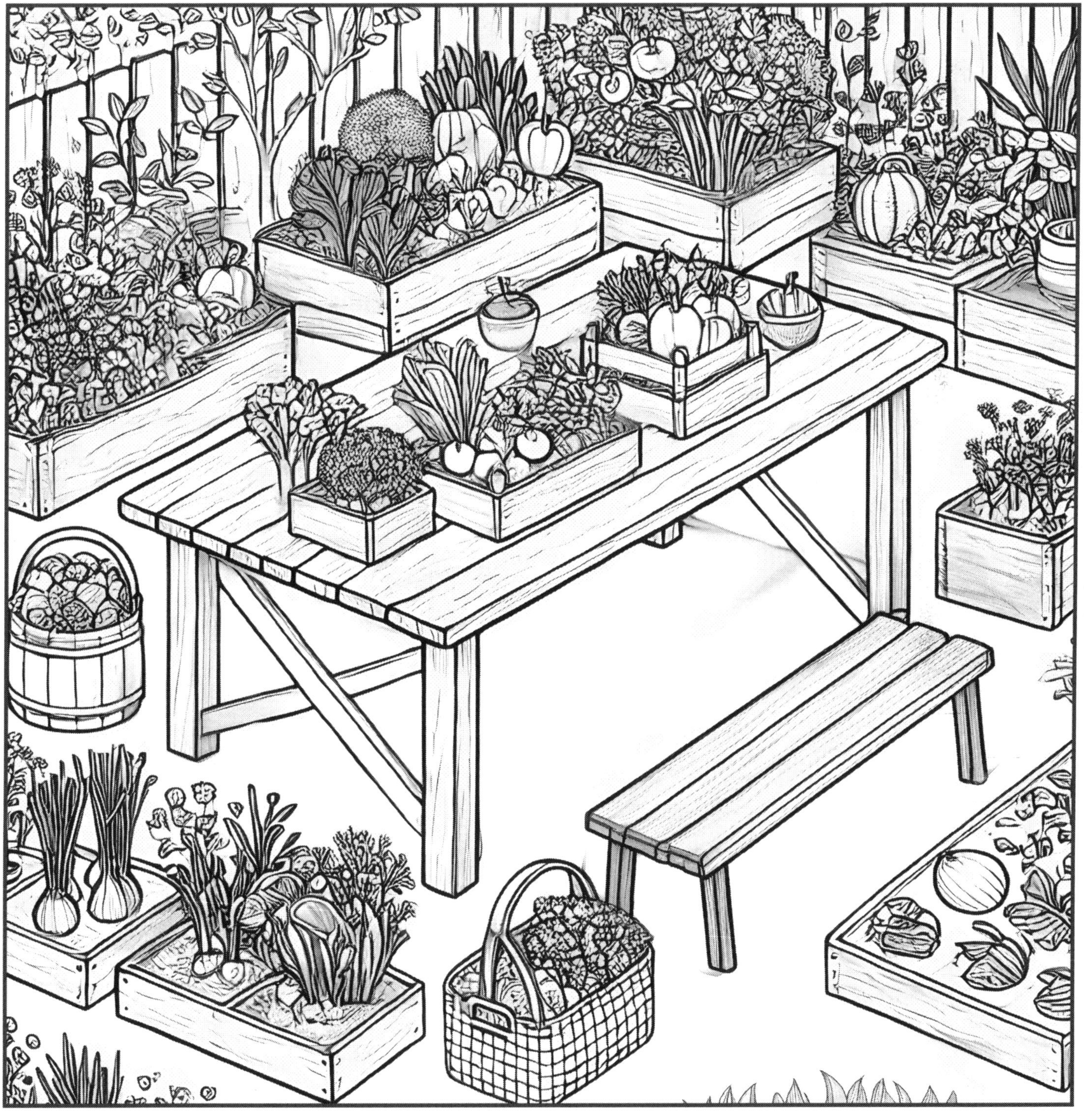

THIS BLACK PAGE IS INTENTIONALLY PLACED TO ENSURE NO BLEED-THROUGH TO THE NEXT PAGE.

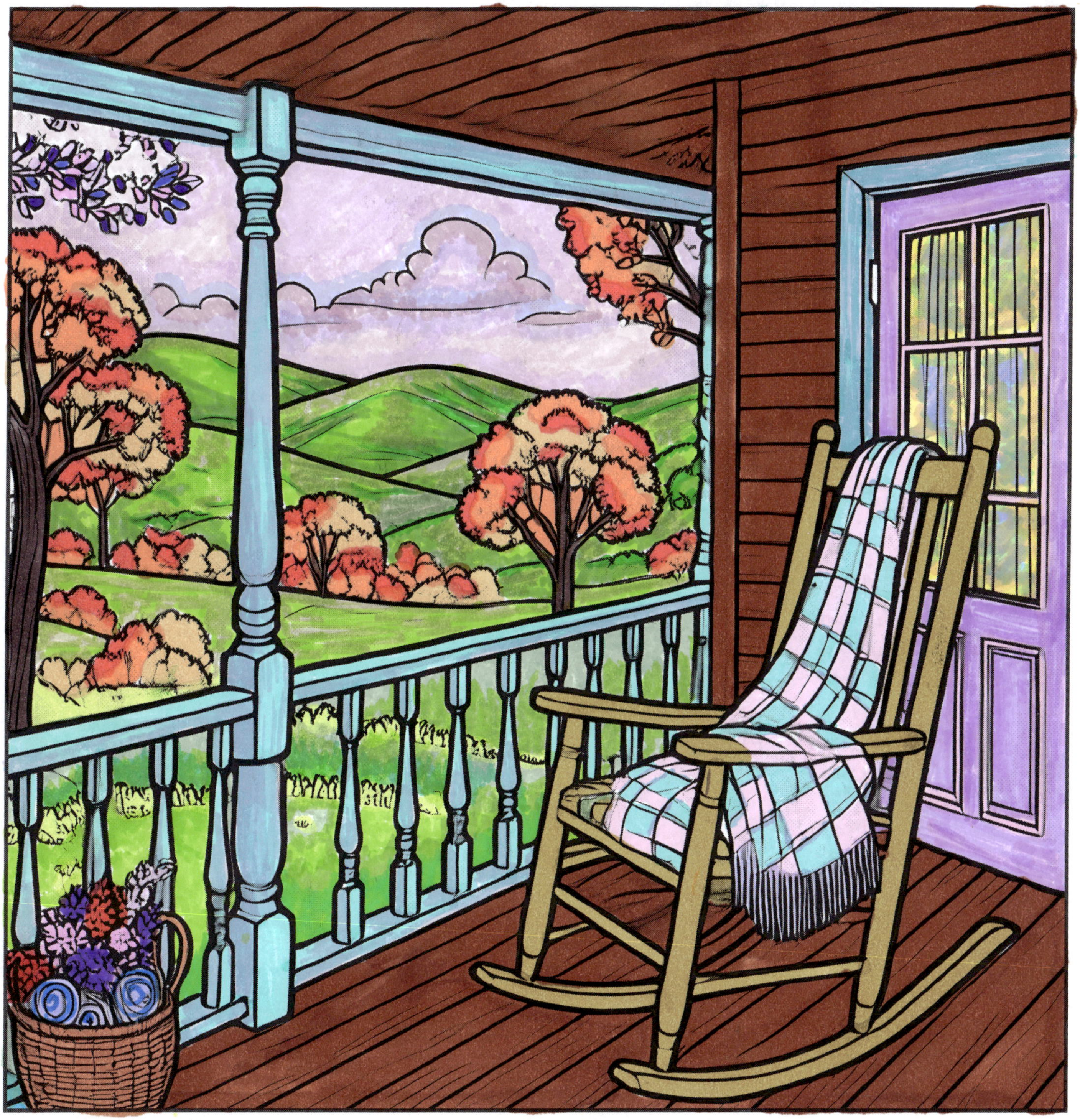

THIS BLACK PAGE IS INTENTIONALLY PLACED TO ENSURE NO BLEED-THROUGH TO THE NEXT PAGE.

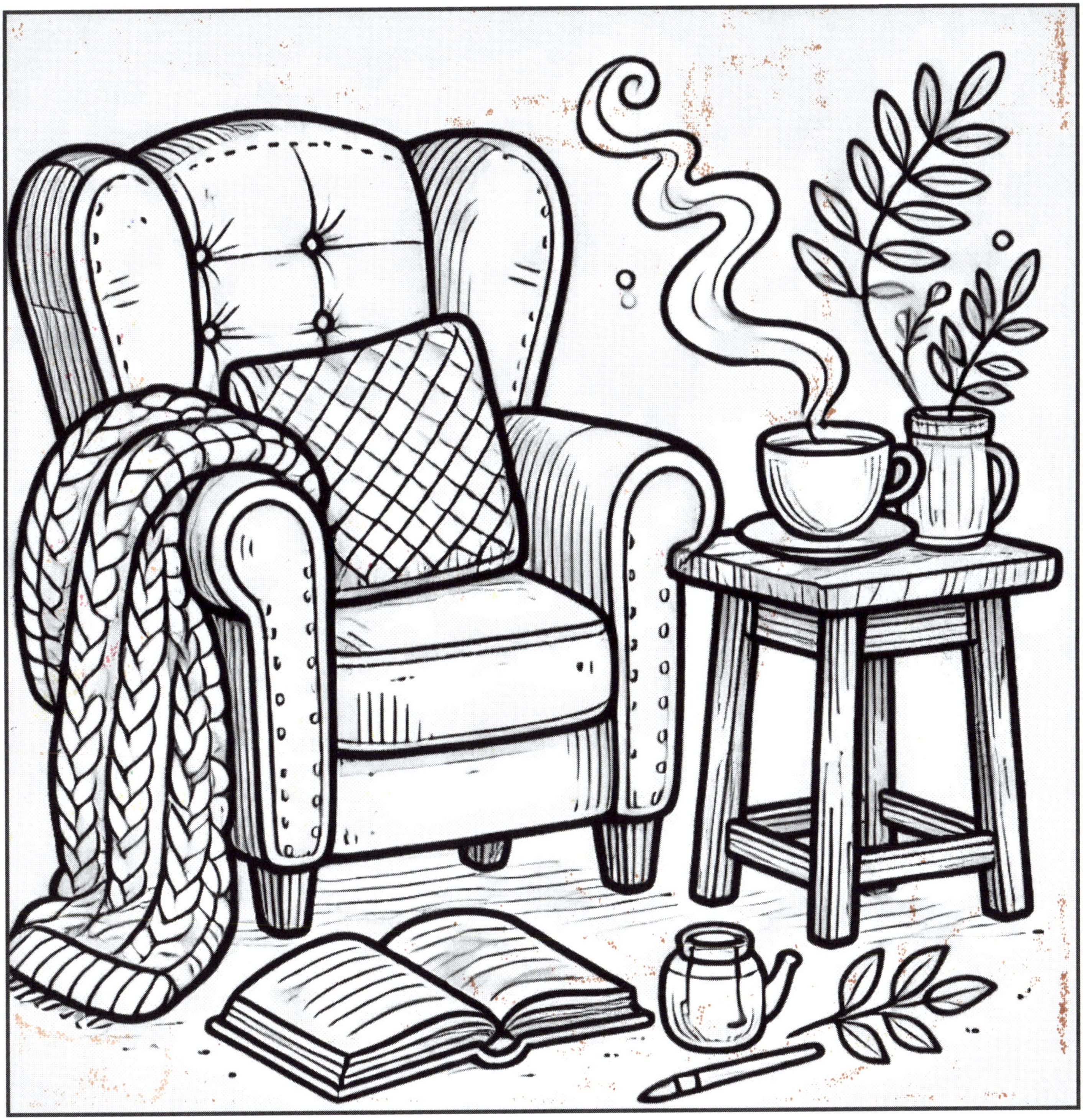

THIS BLACK PAGE IS INTENTIONALLY PLACED TO ENSURE NO BLEED-THROUGH TO THE NEXT PAGE.

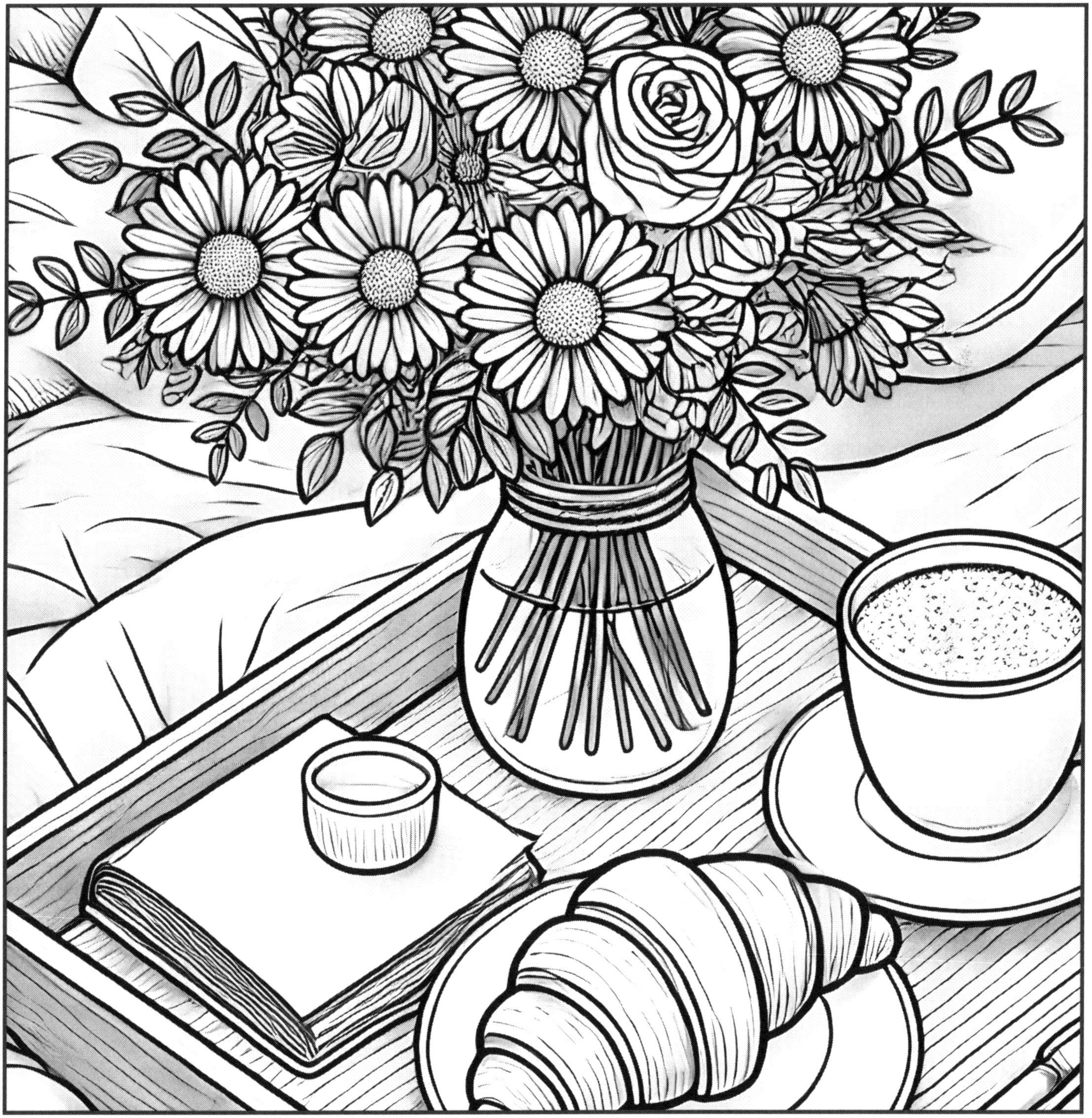

THIS BLACK PAGE IS INTENTIONALLY PLACED TO ENSURE NO BLEED-THROUGH TO THE NEXT PAGE.

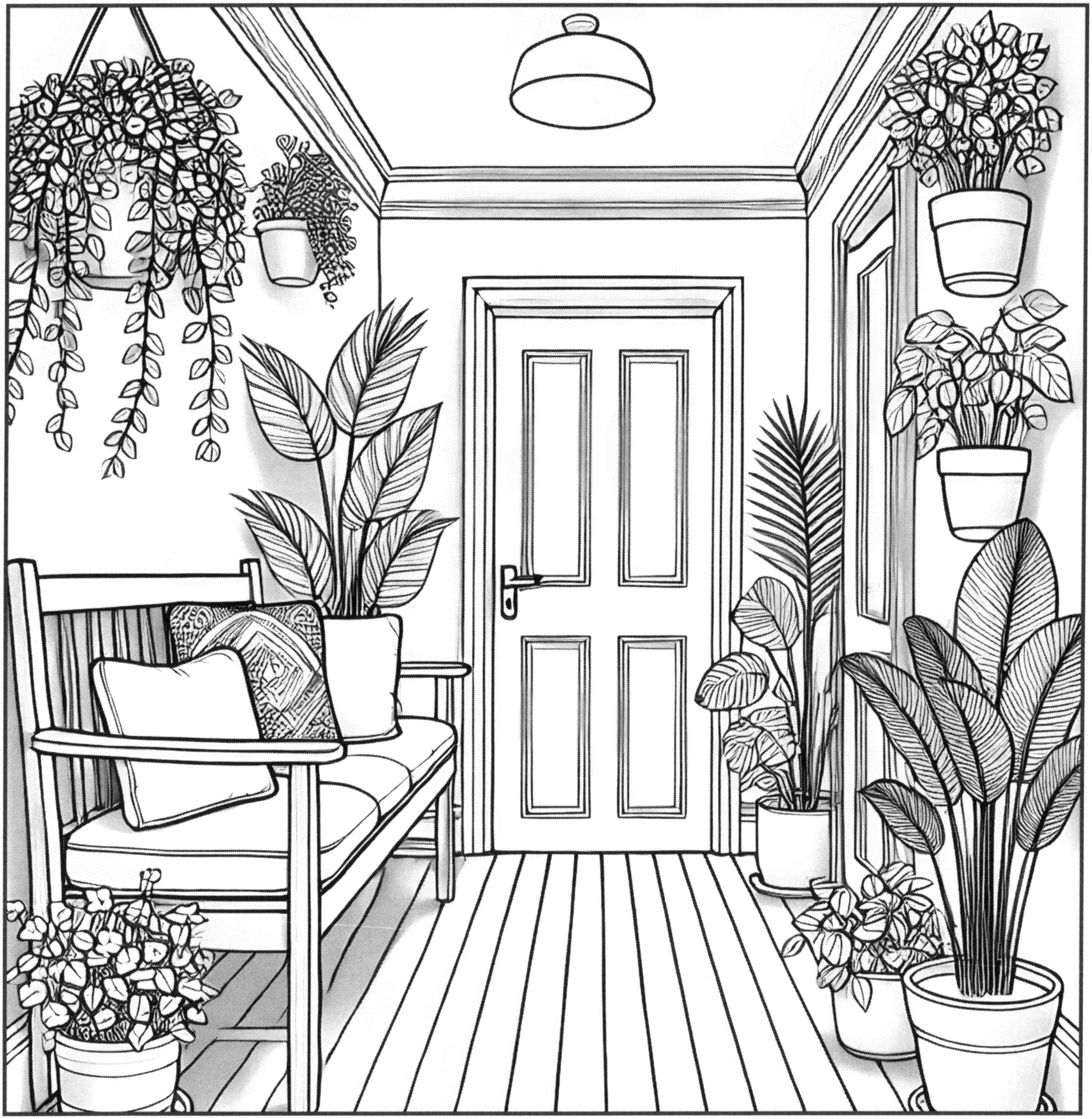

THIS BLACK PAGE IS INTENTIONALLY PLACED TO ENSURE NO BLEED-THROUGH TO THE NEXT PAGE.

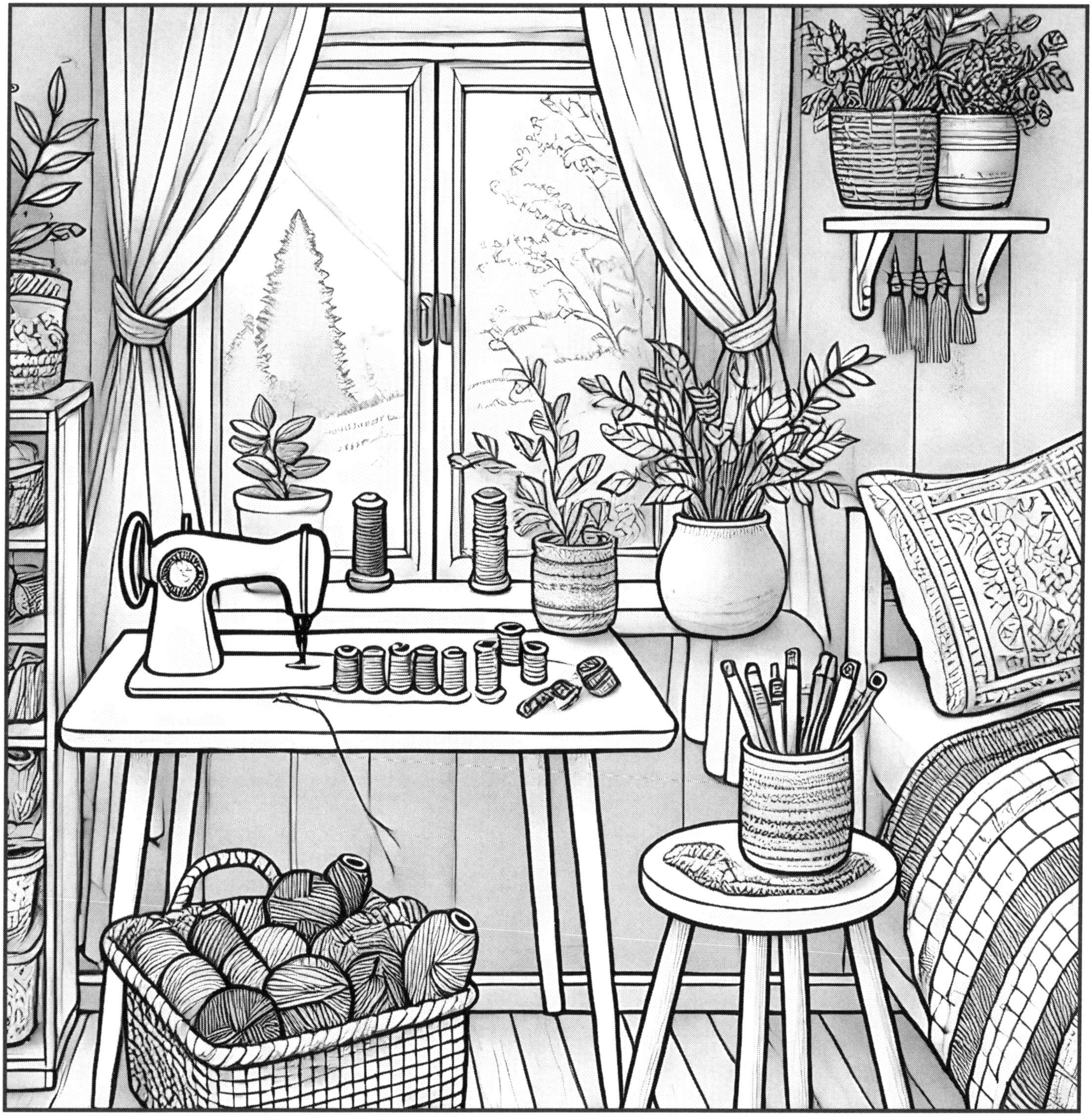

THIS BLACK PAGE IS INTENTIONALLY PLACED TO ENSURE NO BLEED-THROUGH TO THE NEXT PAGE.

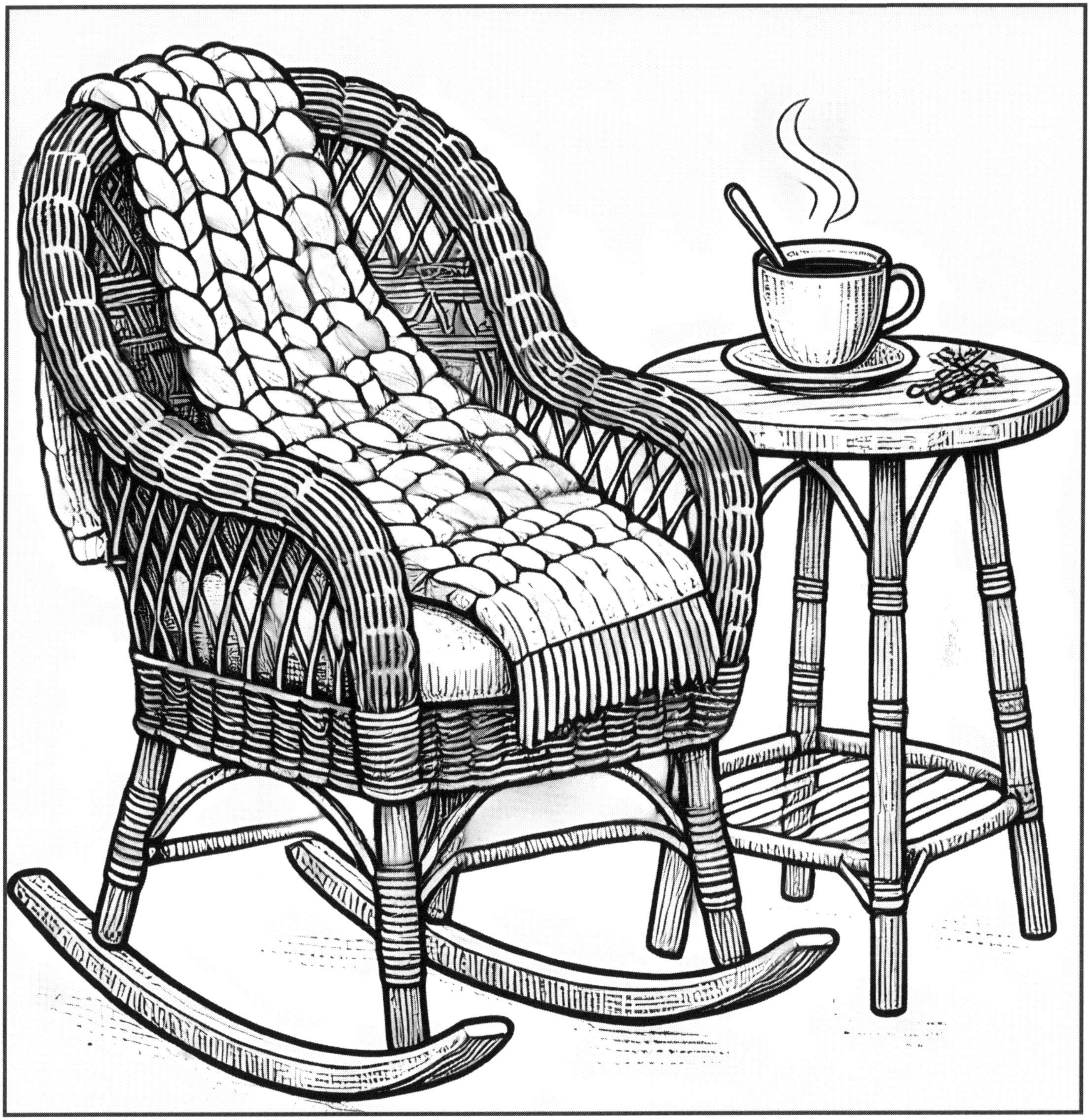

THIS BLACK PAGE IS INTENTIONALLY PLACED TO ENSURE NO BLEED-THROUGH TO THE NEXT PAGE.

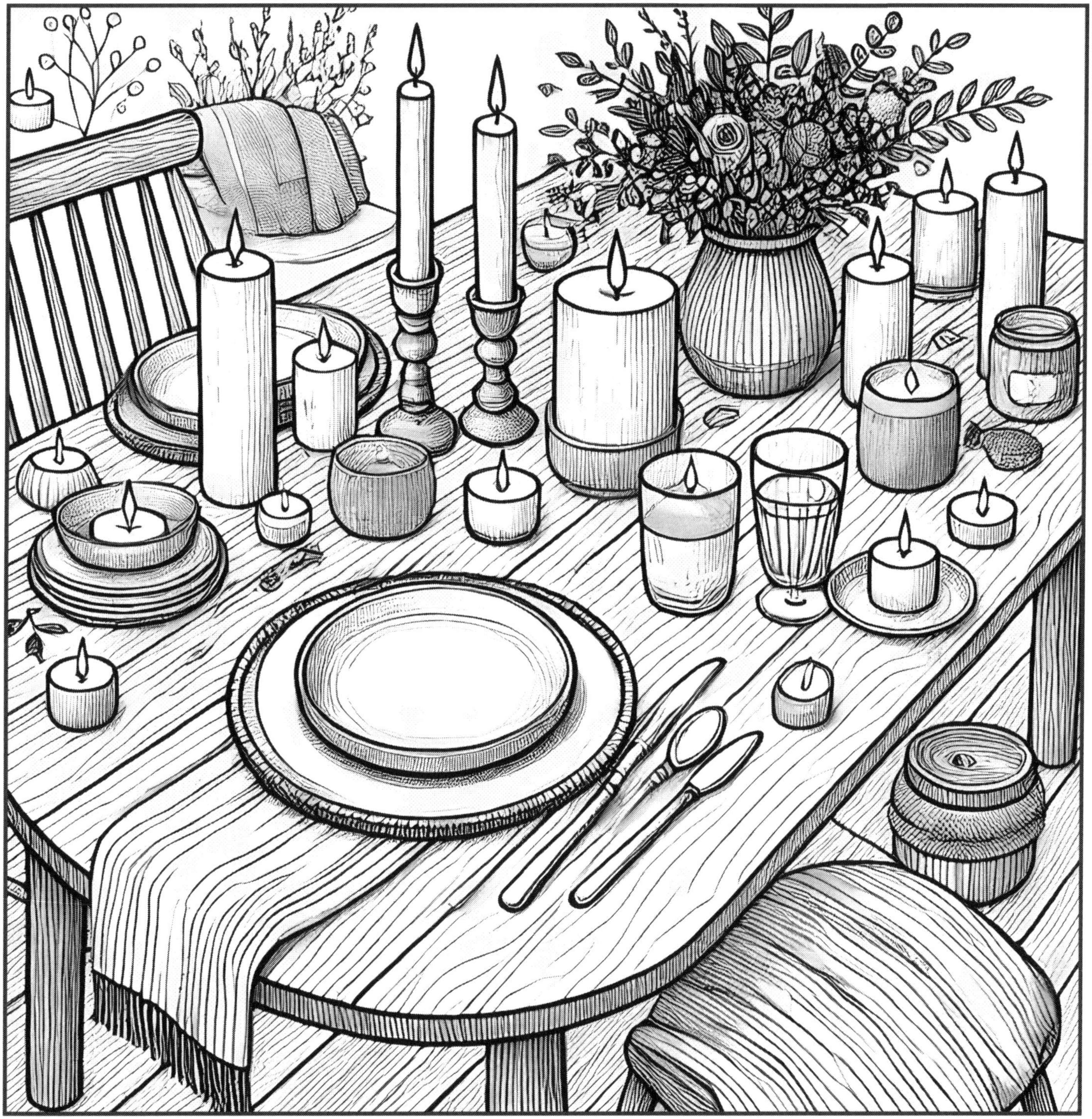

THIS BLACK PAGE IS INTENTIONALLY PLACED TO ENSURE NO BLEED-THROUGH TO THE NEXT PAGE.

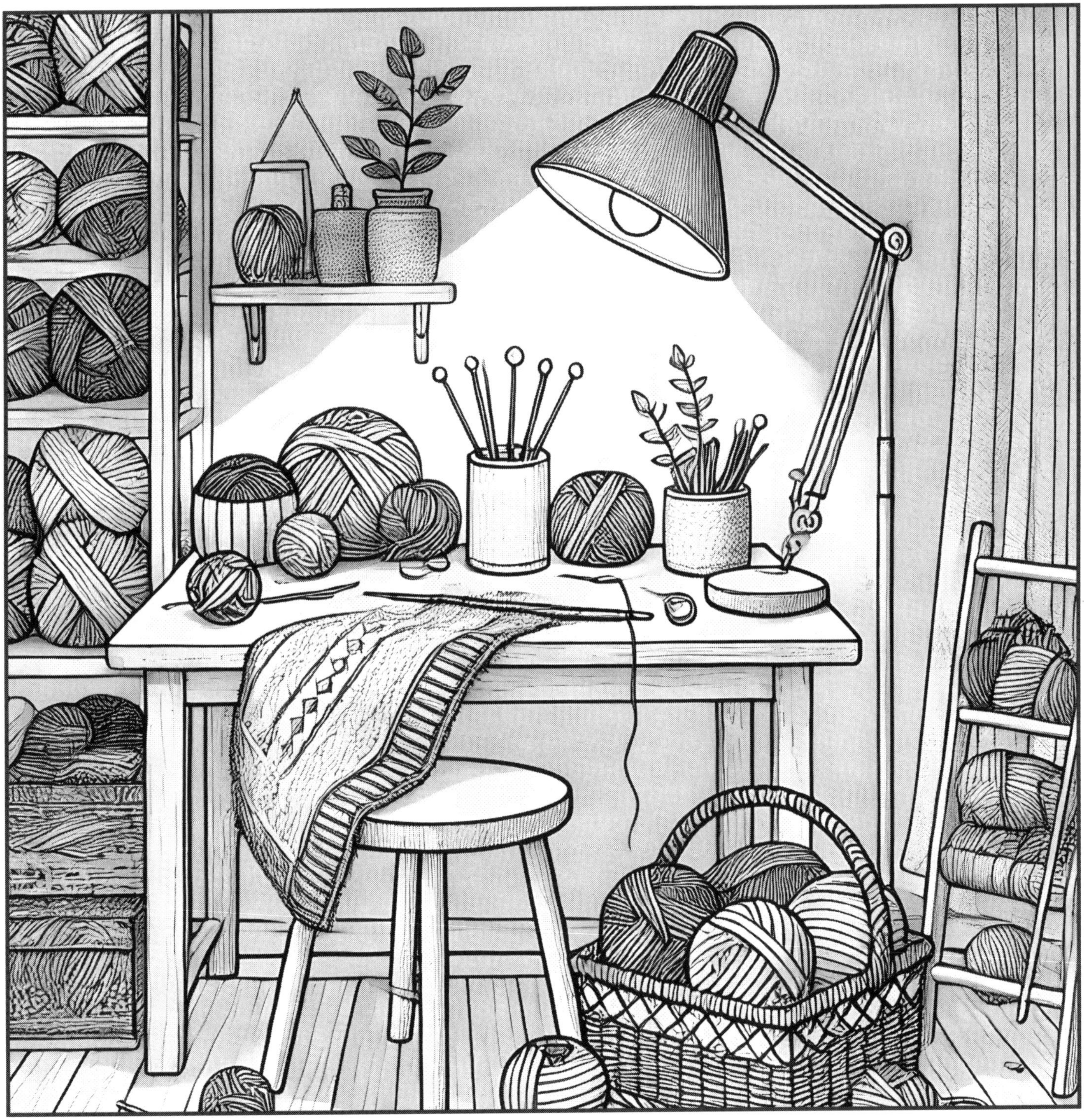

THIS BLACK PAGE IS INTENTIONALLY PLACED TO ENSURE NO BLEED-THROUGH TO THE NEXT PAGE.

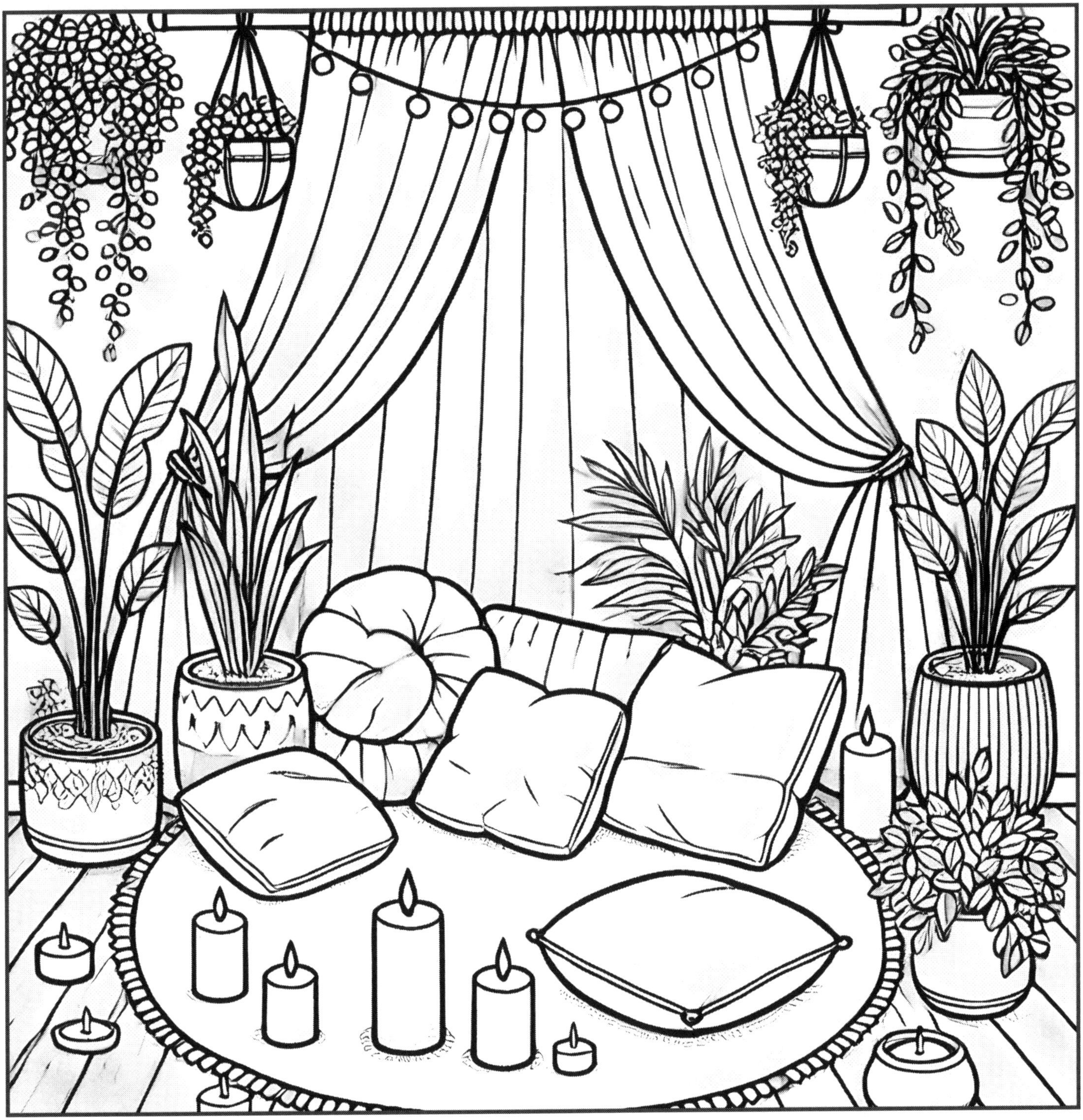

THIS BLACK PAGE IS INTENTIONALLY PLACED TO ENSURE NO BLEED-THROUGH TO THE NEXT PAGE.

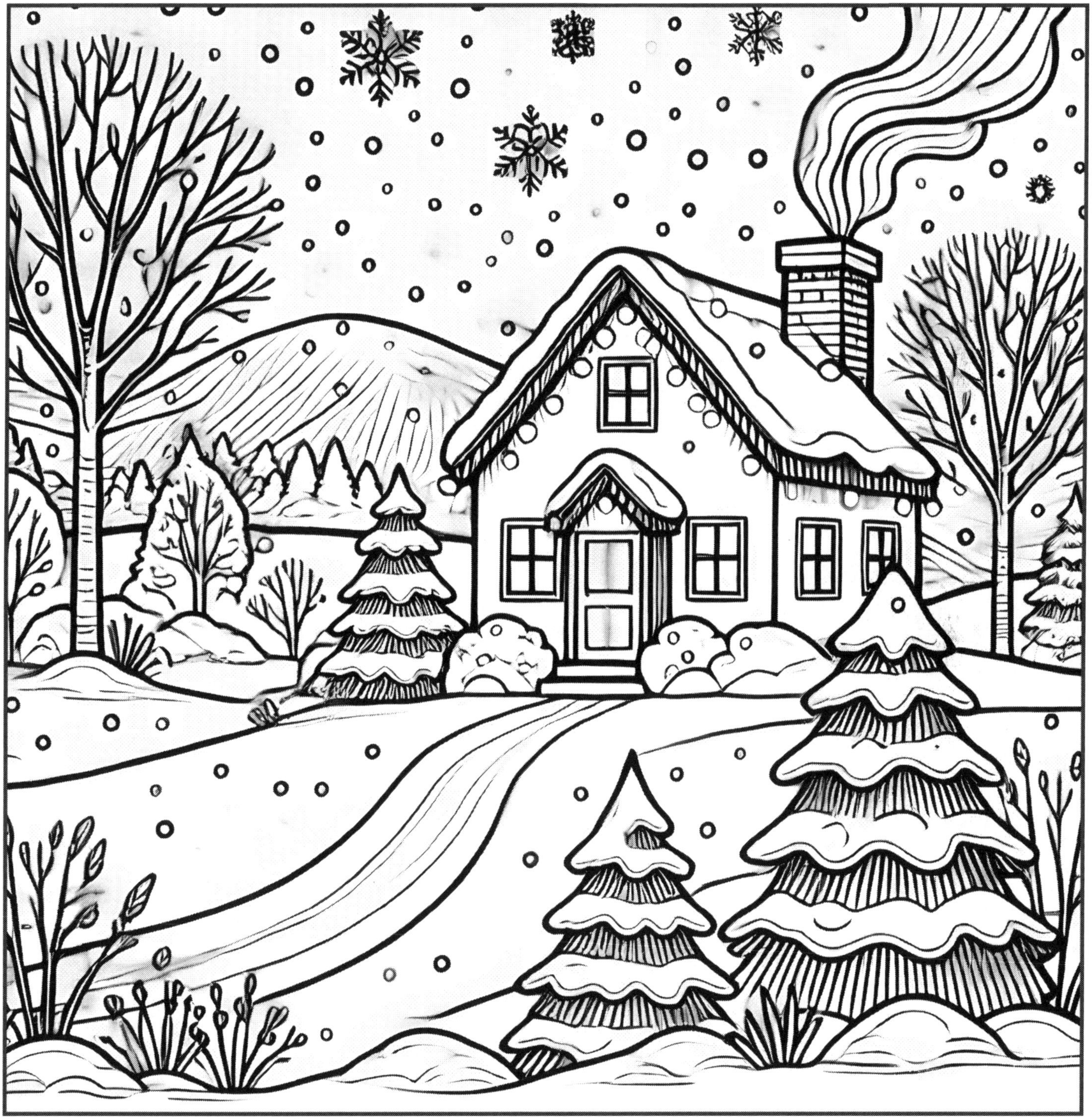

THIS BLACK PAGE IS INTENTIONALLY PLACED TO
ENSURE NO BLEED-THROUGH TO THE NEXT PAGE.

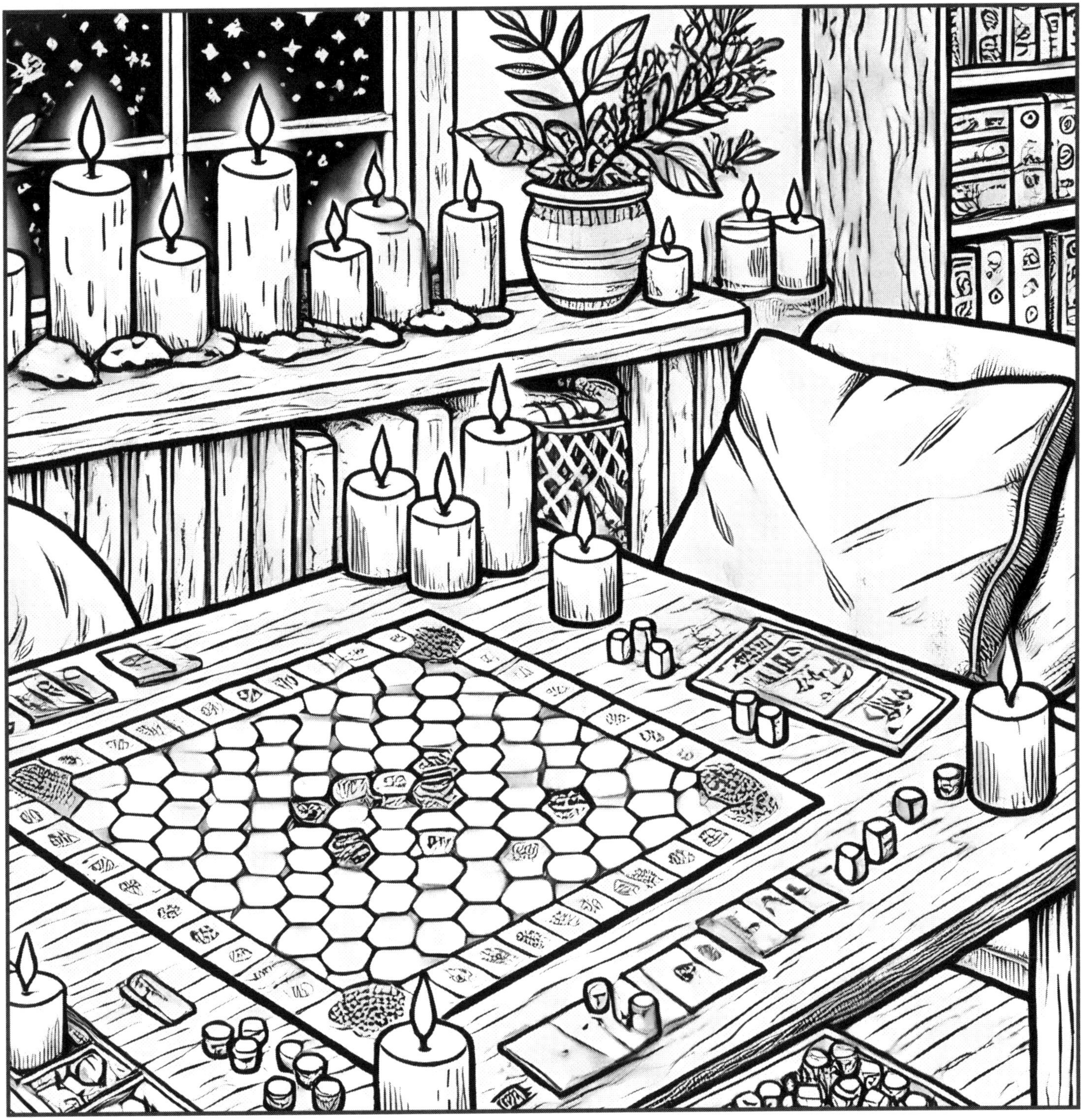

THIS BLACK PAGE IS INTENTIONALLY PLACED TO ENSURE NO BLEED-THROUGH TO THE NEXT PAGE.

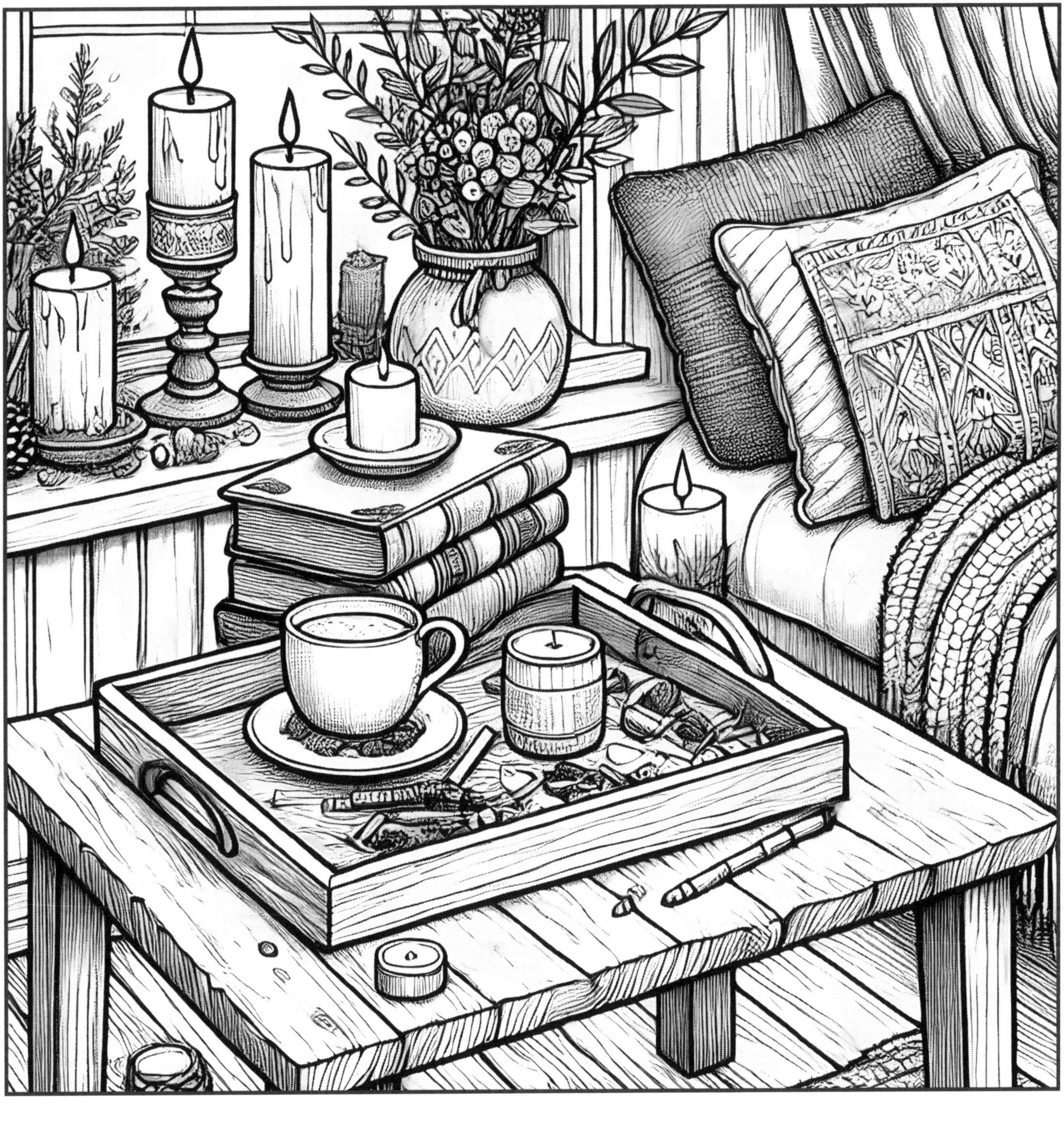

THIS BLACK PAGE IS INTENTIONALLY PLACED TO
ENSURE NO BLEED-THROUGH TO THE NEXT PAGE.

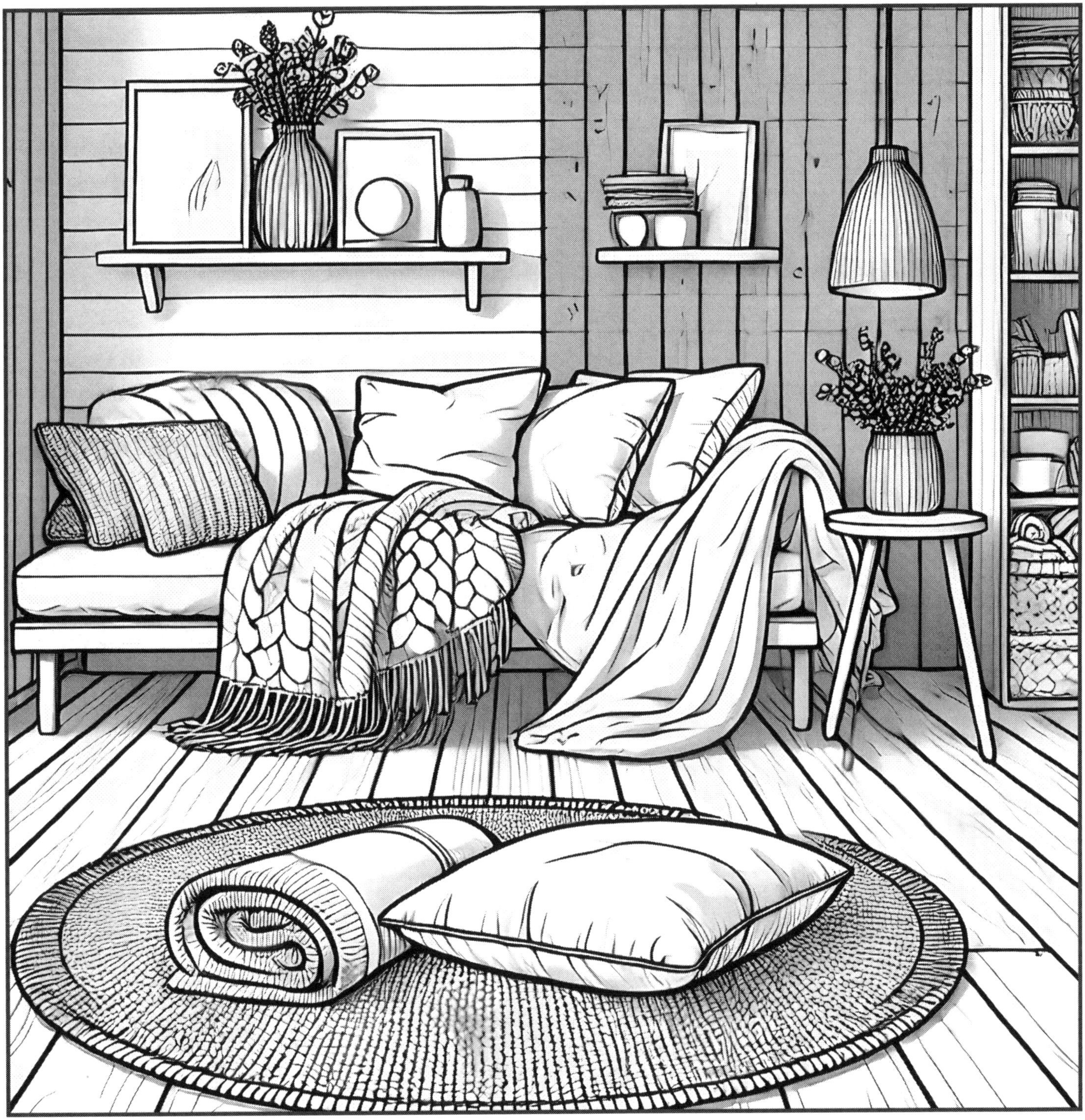

THIS BLACK PAGE IS INTENTIONALLY PLACED TO ENSURE NO BLEED-THROUGH TO THE NEXT PAGE.

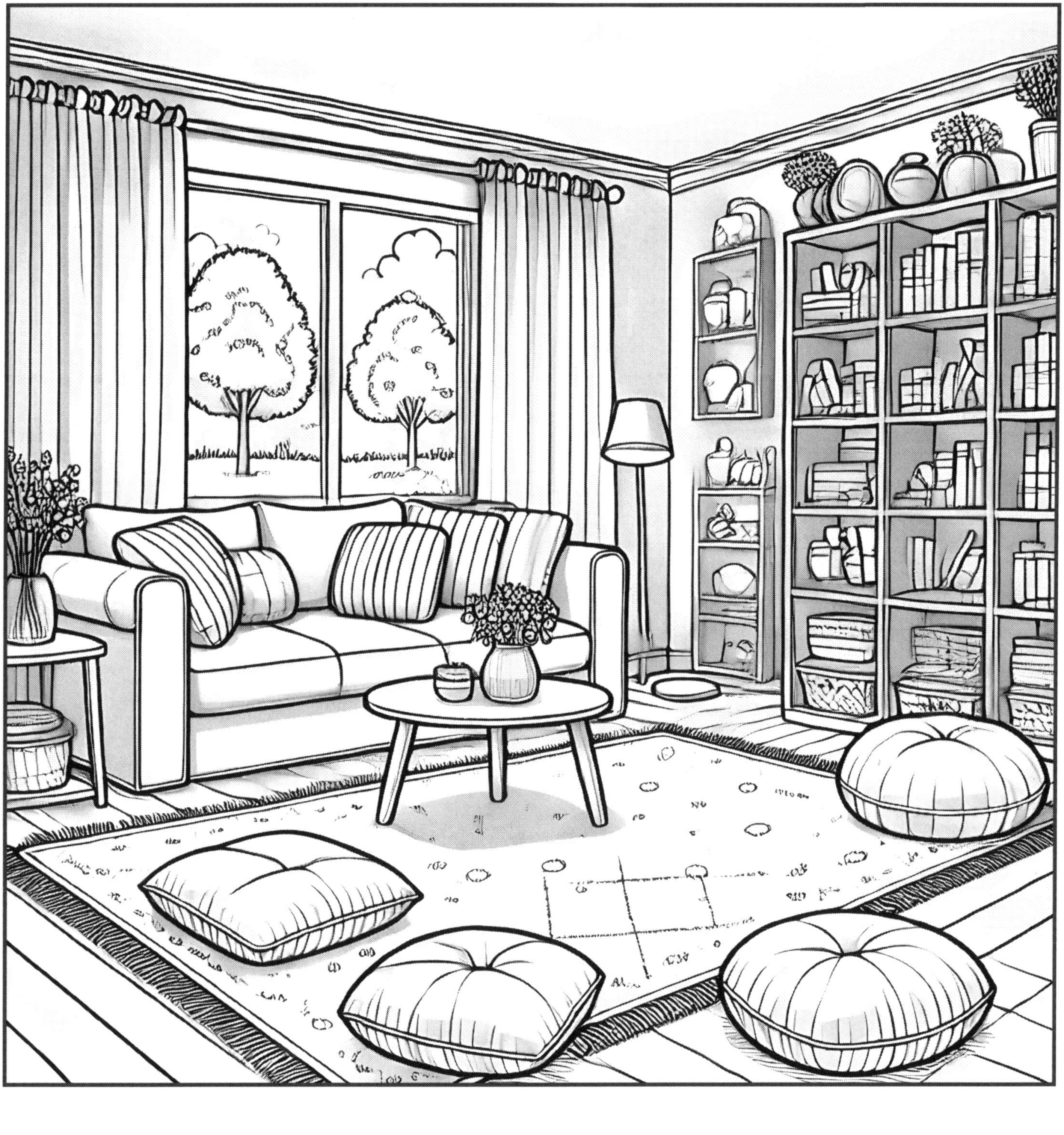

THIS BLACK PAGE IS INTENTIONALLY PLACED TO ENSURE NO BLEED-THROUGH TO THE NEXT PAGE.

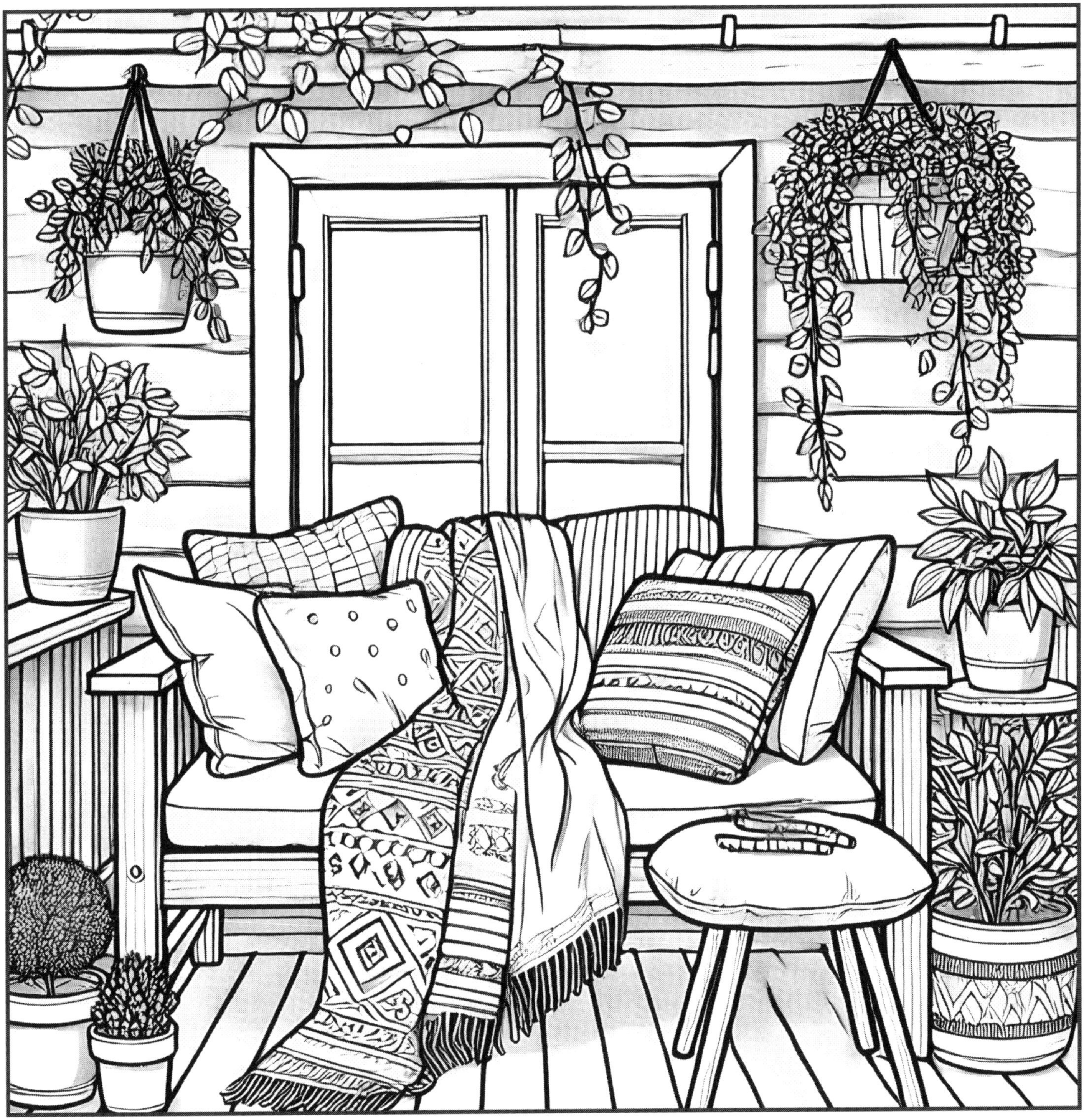

THIS BLACK PAGE IS INTENTIONALLY PLACED TO
ENSURE NO BLEED-THROUGH TO THE NEXT PAGE.

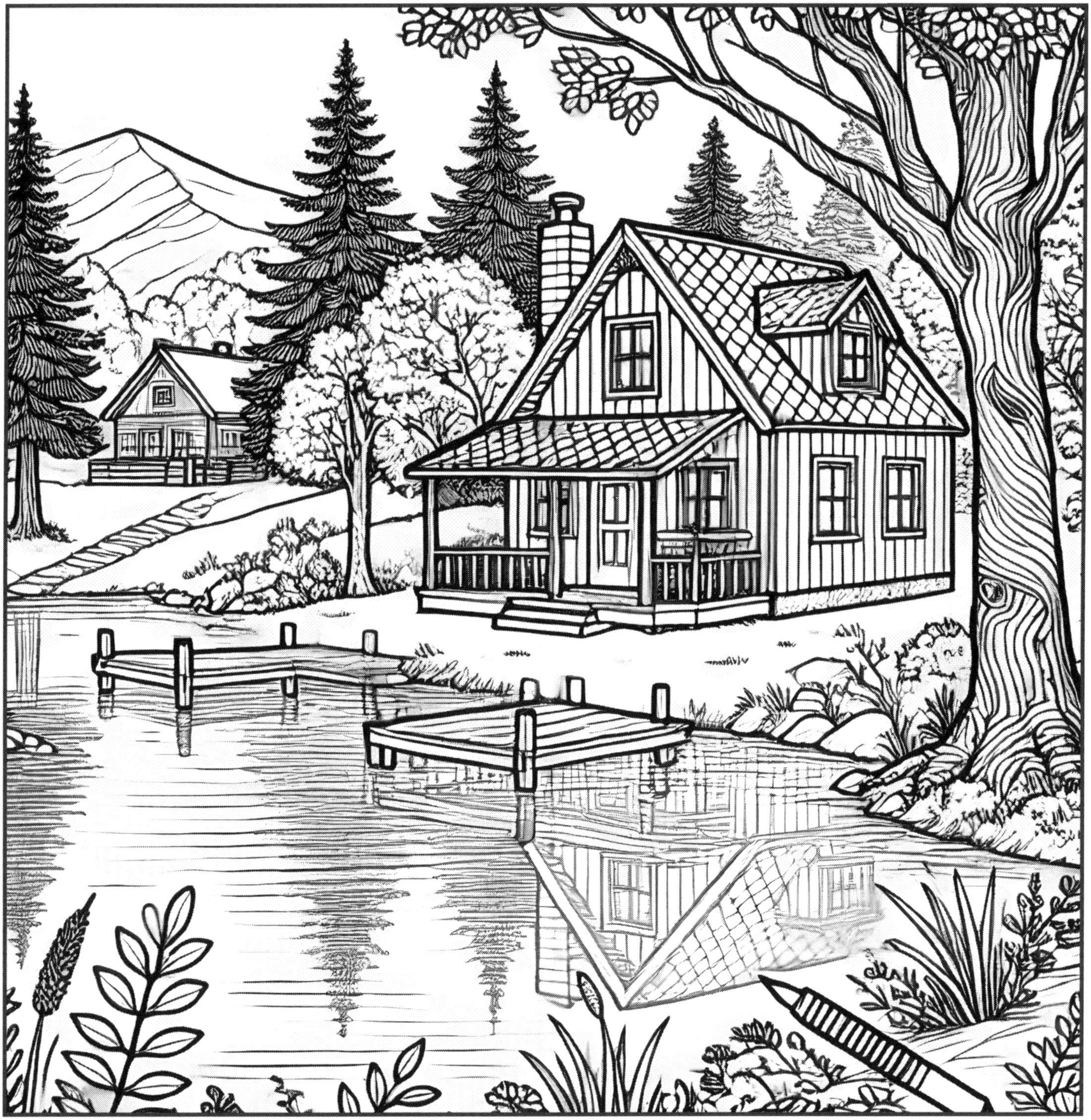

THIS BLACK PAGE IS INTENTIONALLY PLACED TO ENSURE NO BLEED-THROUGH TO THE NEXT PAGE.

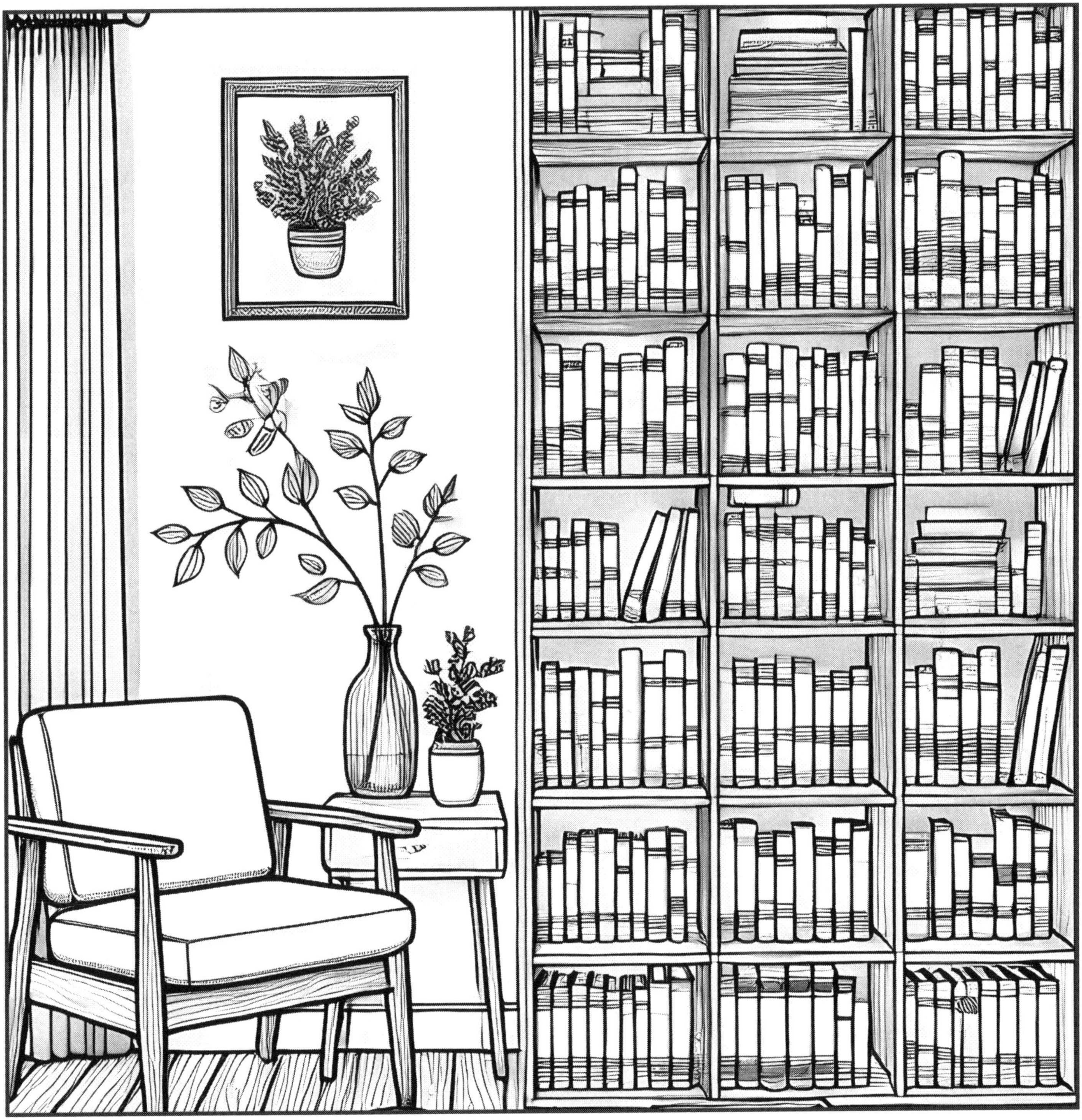

THIS BLACK PAGE IS INTENTIONALLY PLACED TO
ENSURE NO BLEED-THROUGH TO THE NEXT PAGE.

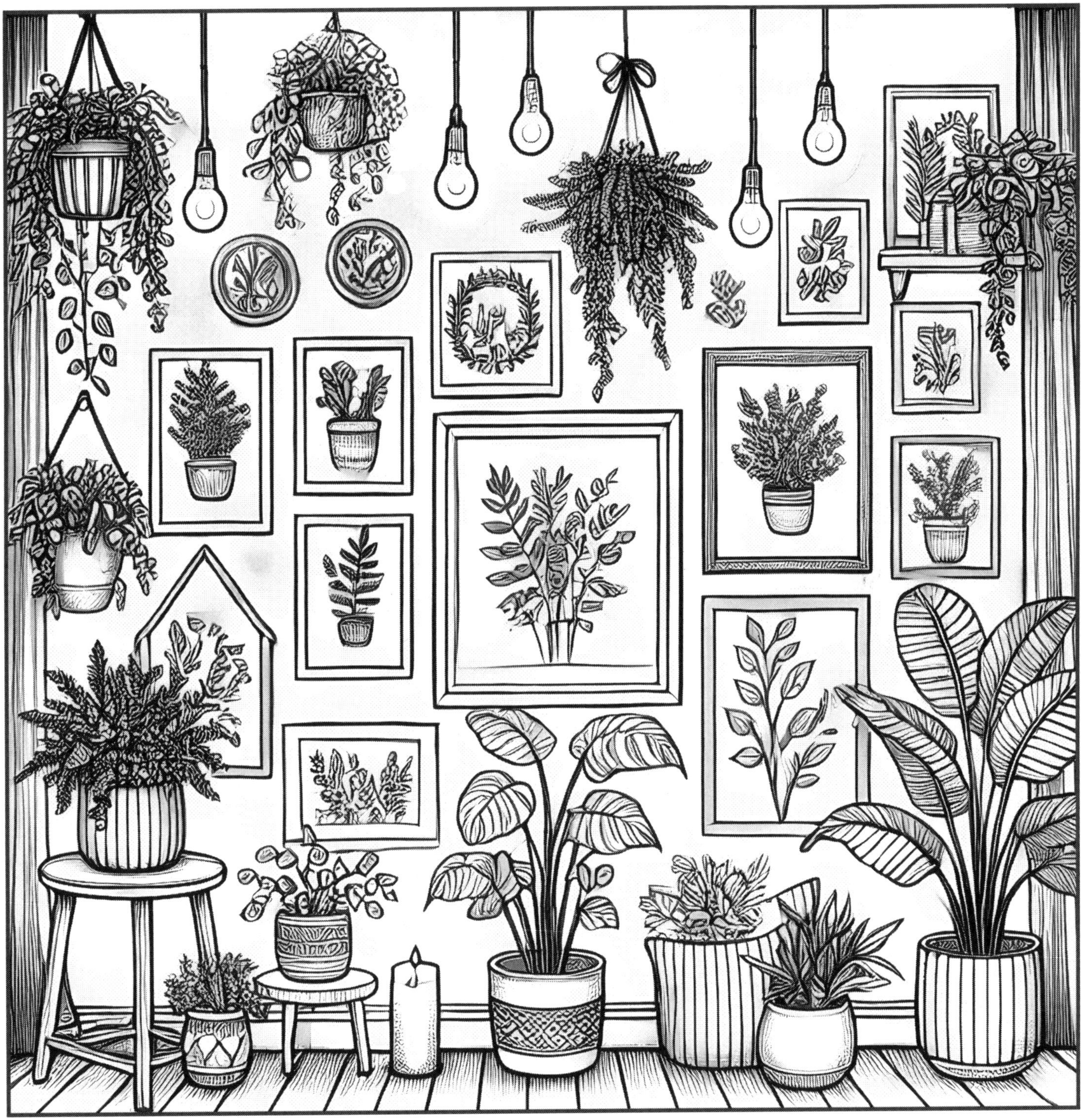

THIS BLACK PAGE IS INTENTIONALLY PLACED TO ENSURE NO BLEED-THROUGH TO THE NEXT PAGE.

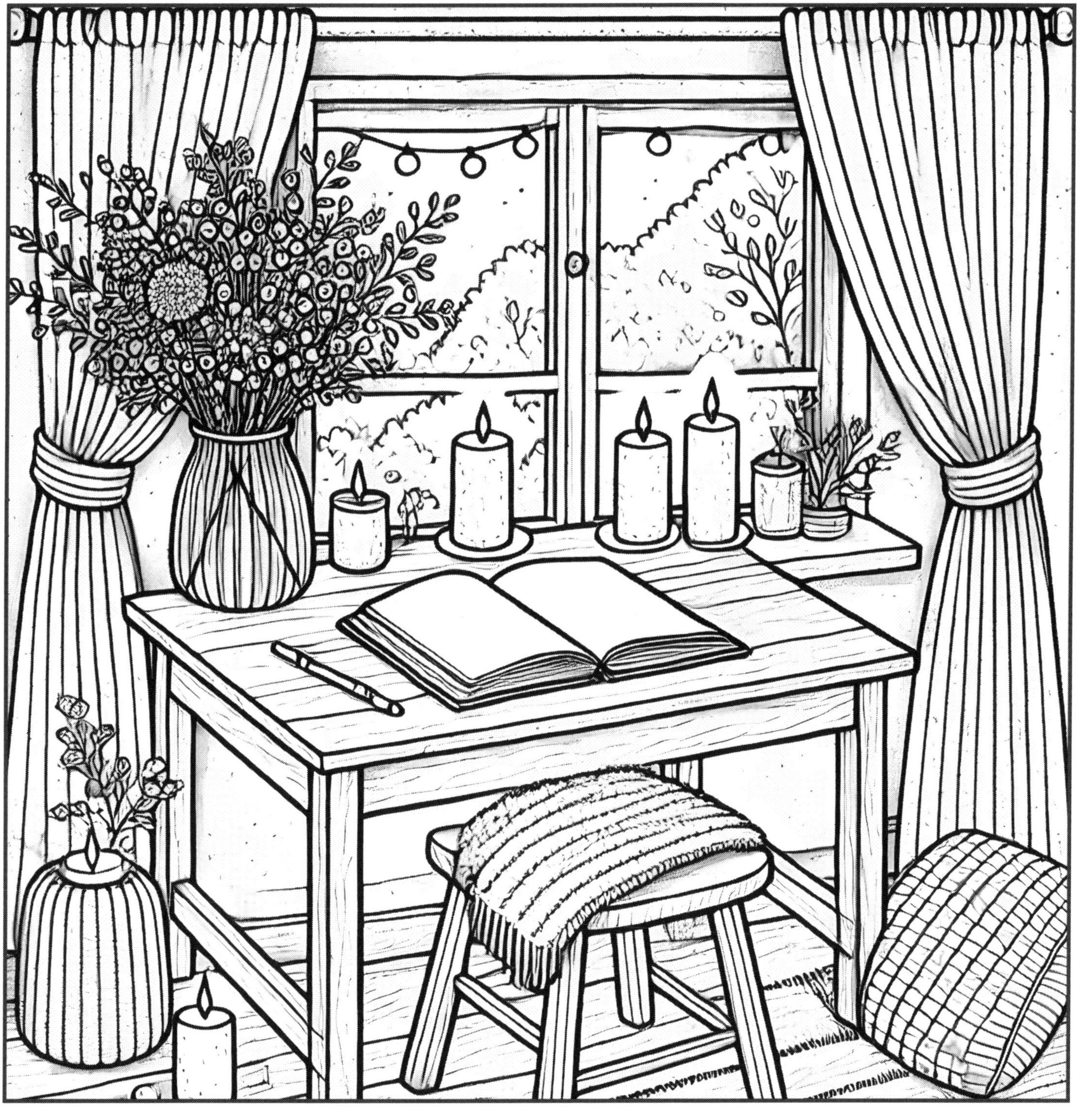

THIS BLACK PAGE IS INTENTIONALLY PLACED TO ENSURE NO BLEED-THROUGH TO THE NEXT PAGE.

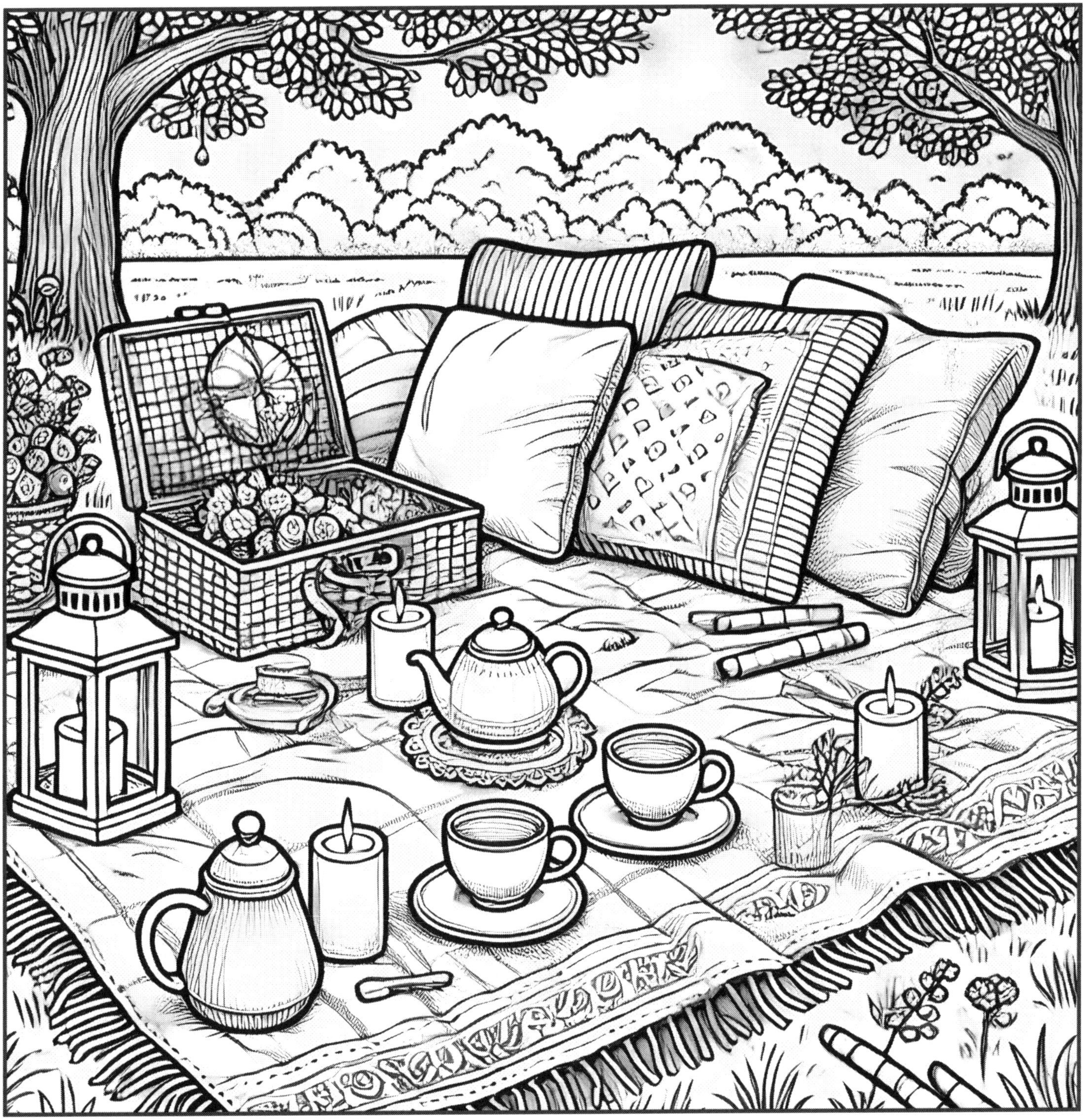

THIS BLACK PAGE IS INTENTIONALLY PLACED TO ENSURE NO BLEED-THROUGH TO THE NEXT PAGE.

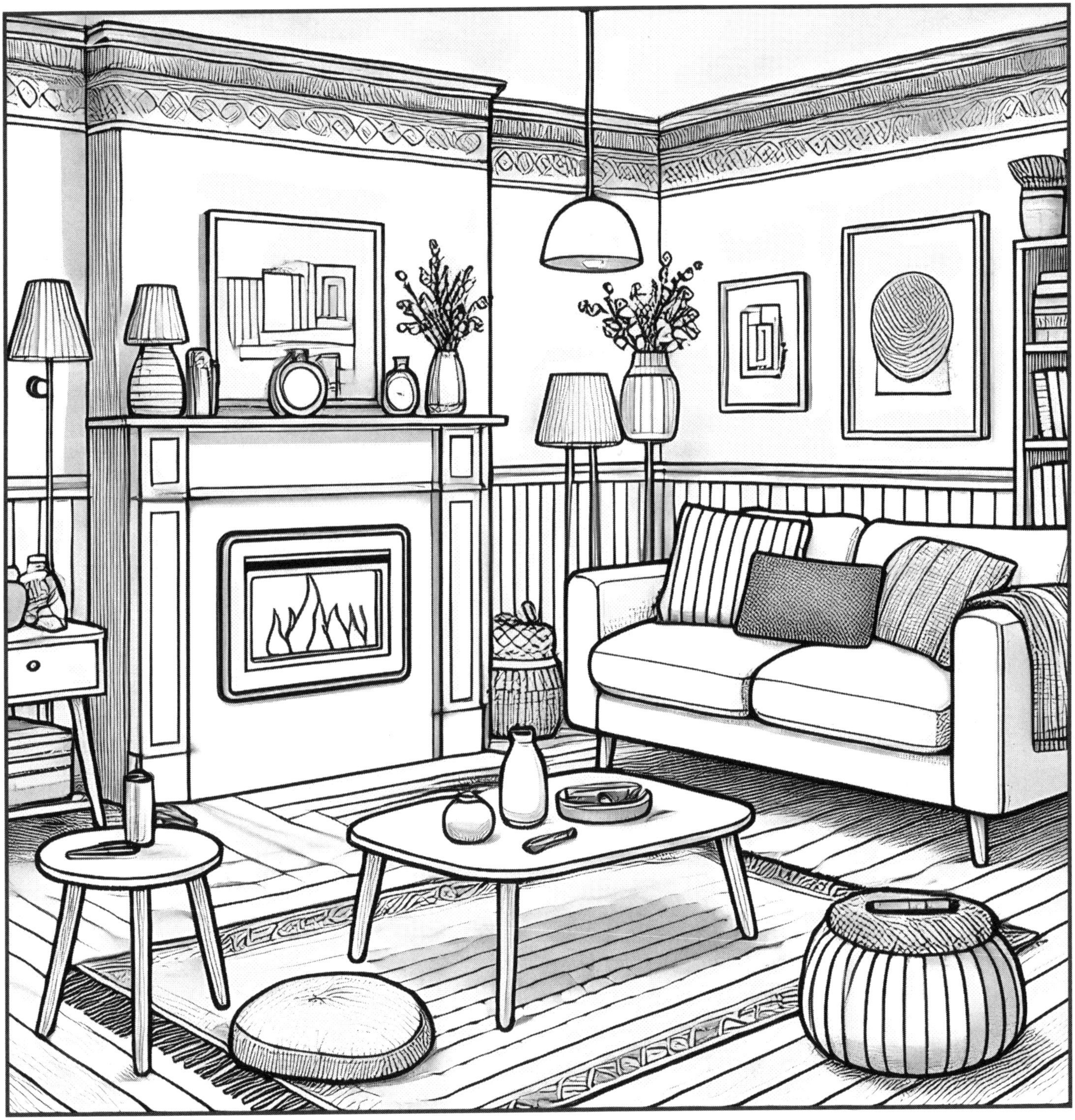

THIS BLACK PAGE IS INTENTIONALLY PLACED TO ENSURE NO BLEED-THROUGH TO THE NEXT PAGE.

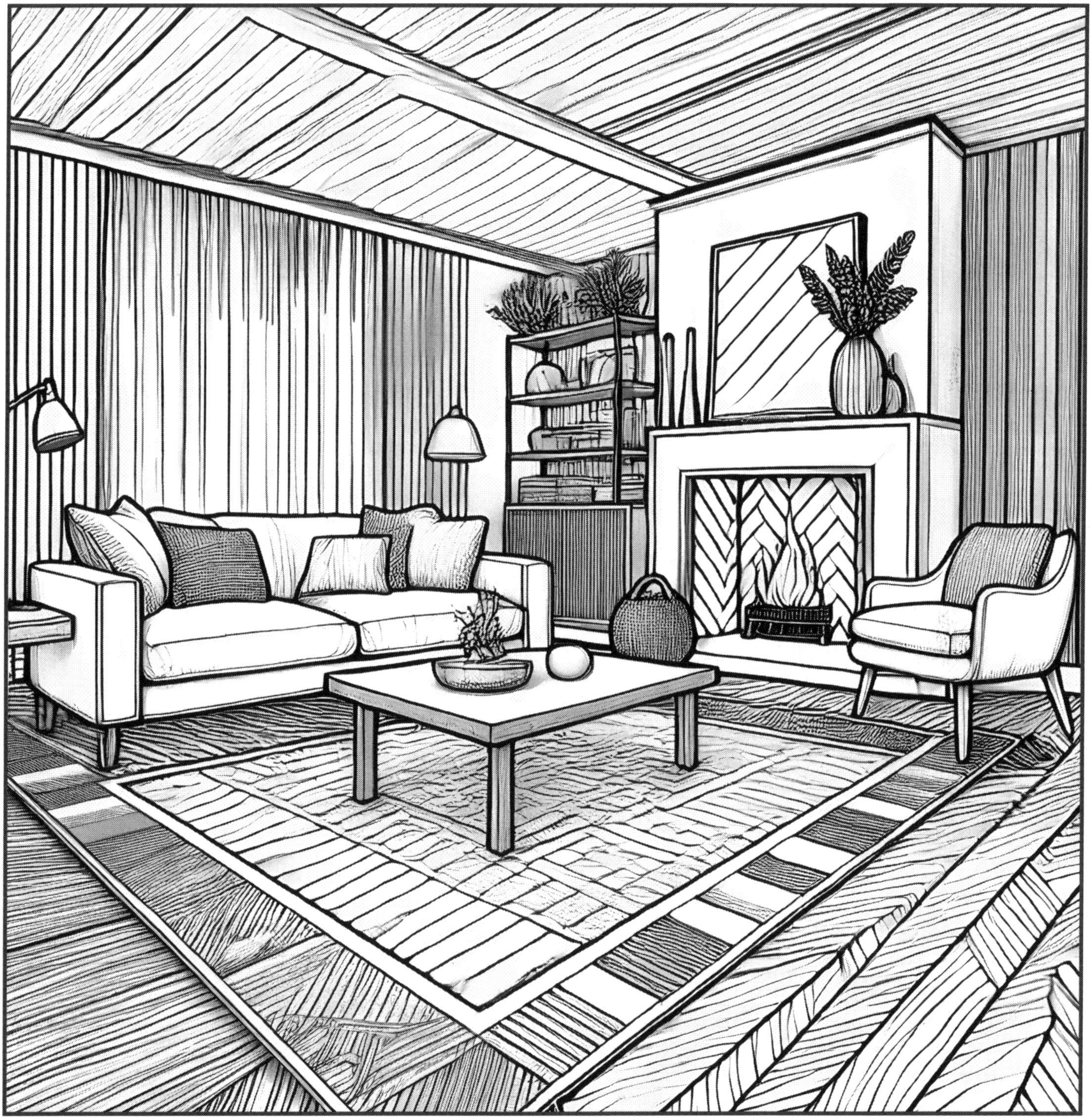

THIS BLACK PAGE IS INTENTIONALLY PLACED TO
ENSURE NO BLEED-THROUGH TO THE NEXT PAGE.

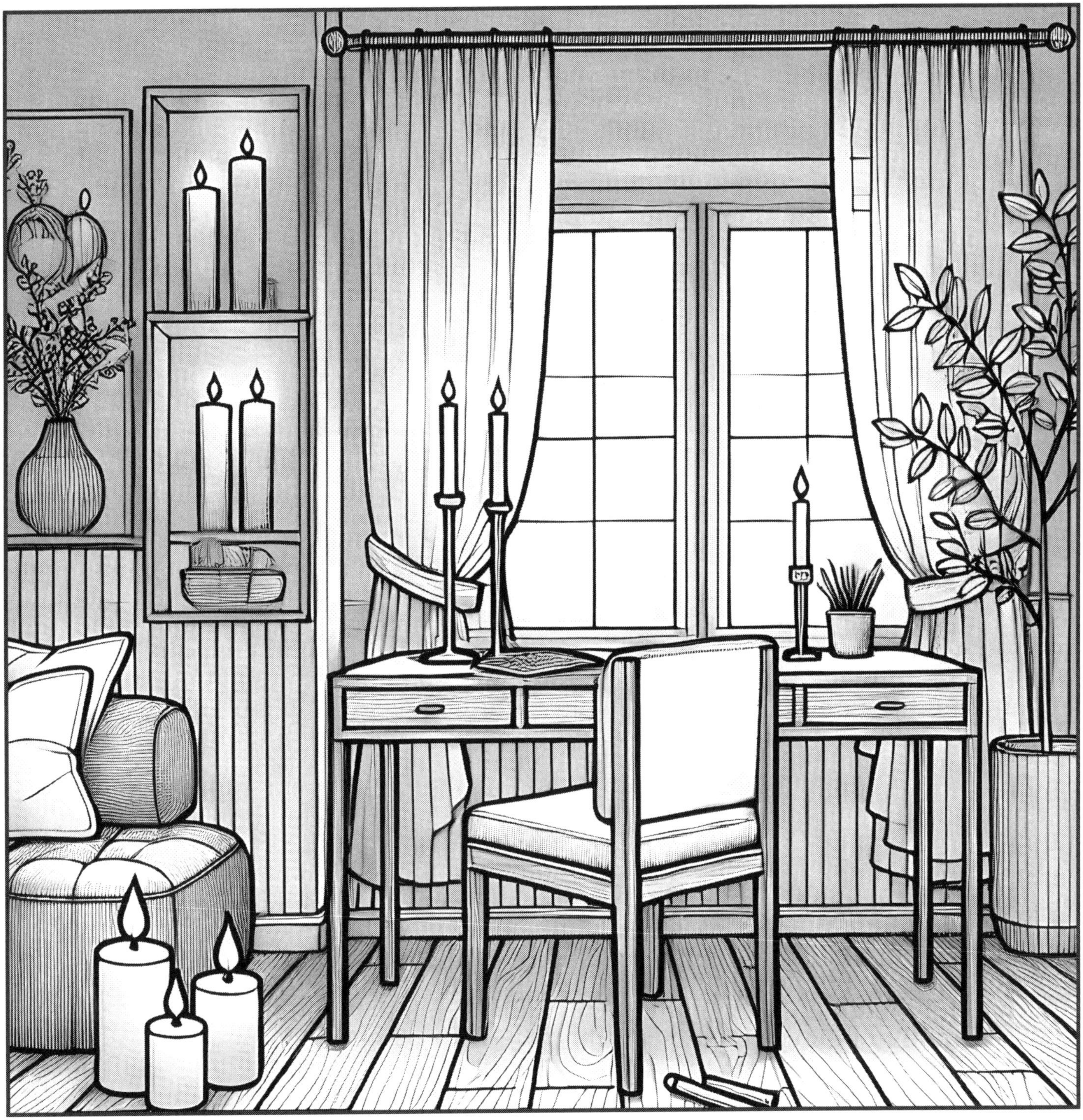

THIS BLACK PAGE IS INTENTIONALLY PLACED TO ENSURE NO BLEED-THROUGH TO THE NEXT PAGE.

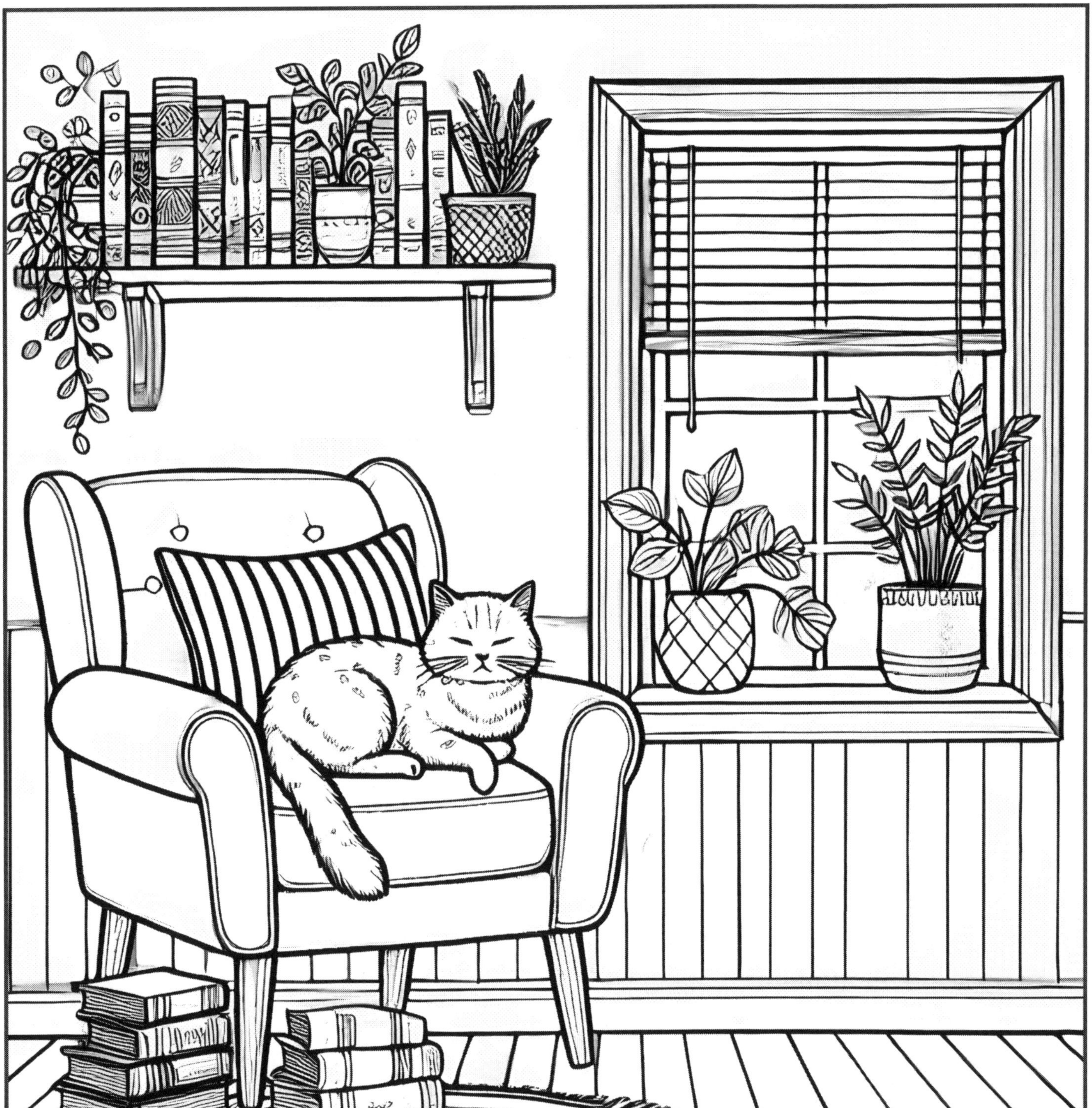

THIS BLACK PAGE IS INTENTIONALLY PLACED TO ENSURE NO BLEED-THROUGH TO THE NEXT PAGE.

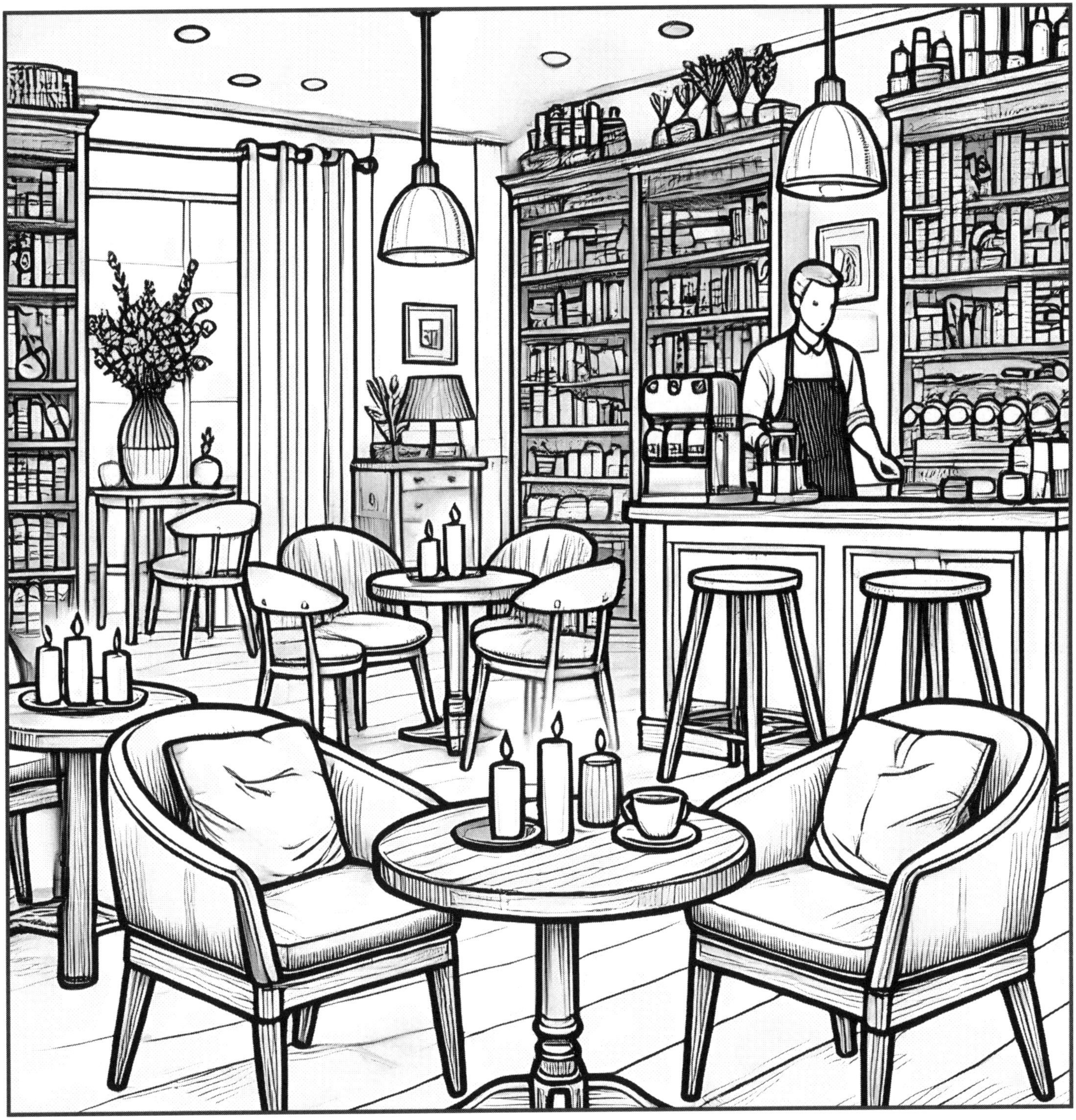

THIS BLACK PAGE IS INTENTIONALLY PLACED TO
ENSURE NO BLEED-THROUGH TO THE NEXT PAGE.

THANK YOU!

DEAR CUSTOMER,

THANK YOU FOR YOUR PURCHASE! WE REALLY APPRECIATE YOUR SUPPORT AND TRUST IN OUR COMPANY. YOUR DECISION TO CHOOSE OUR PRODUCT MEANS A LOT TO US.

WE SINCERELY ASK YOU TO SHARE YOUR HONEST OPINION ABOUT YOUR EXPERIENCE WITH OUR PRODUCT ON AMAZON. YOUR FEEDBACK WILL NOT ONLY HELP US IMPROVE, BUT ALSO HELP OTHER POTENTIAL CUSTOMERS MAKE INFORMED DECISIONS.

WE ARE A SMALL COMPANY, SO EVERY REVIEW IS EXTREMELY IMPORTANT TO US. YOUR HONEST REVIEW WILL NOT ONLY HELP US GROW, BUT ALSO ALLOW US TO CREATE EVEN BETTER PRODUCTS IN THE FUTURE. WE BELIEVE THAT CONSTRUCTIVE FEEDBACK IS ESSENTIAL TO OUR DEVELOPMENT, AND YOUR INSIGHTS PLAY A KEY ROLE IN SHAPING OUR OFFERINGS.

THANK YOU AGAIN FOR BEING A PART OF OUR JOURNEY. WE ARE GRATEFUL FOR YOUR SUPPORT AND LOOK FORWARD TO YOUR FEEDBACK.

Printed in Great Britain
by Amazon